Reminiscence and lifelong learning

niace

promoting adult learning

niace

promoting adult learning

NIACE has a broad remit to promote lifelong learning opportunities for adults. NIACE works to
develop increased participation in education and training, particularly for those who do not have
easy access because of class, gender, age, race, language and culture, learning difficulties or
disabilities, or insufficient financial resources.

ISBN 978 1 86201 248 6

You can find NIACE online at www.niace.org.uk

Cataloguing in Publication Data
A CIP record of this title i

Designed and typeset by P
Printed by Latimer Trend &

Contents

Acknowledgements

Many thanks to everyone who agreed to be photographed for this book, including:
Residents of Lincoln House;
Residents of Shalom;
Members of the William Booth Day Centre;
Members of the Heartsease Lunch Club;
Judy Colman and her gradnchildren Megan and Oliver.

Thanks, too, to everyone who helped with the research by agreeing to be interviewed.

All photography is by Sarah Housden, 2005–06.

Introduction

The central premise of this book is that learners' personal memories represent a rich resource in learning throughout the lifespan, providing an invaluable source of knowledge, ideas and experiences for tutors and fellow learners to draw on and work with. Through sharing their experiences learners can teach each other (and their tutors), as well as inspiring and motivating each other to develop skills in areas other than reminiscing.

This book describes an array of projects and learning situations where, beginning with the sharing of memories, older people have gone on to develop skills in: forming and sustaining relationships; oral and written communication; using modern technology such as computers; arts and crafts; and literacy. Time and again, learners' memories are seen not only as the starting point for gaining new skills, but also as a channel through which those learners grow in confidence, self-esteem and a true sense of their own worth. Placing value on learners' memories enables them to see themselves as people with something to give – a highly significant reversal of the situation in which many retired people find themselves, and one of particular importance for those living in residential care where the usual emphasis is on their needs and what others can do for them. This story would be impressive if it stopped there, but it goes further with many older people finding they have renewed enthusiasm and strength to get more involved in life after taking part in reminiscence, sometimes to the point of being better able to look after themselves, and needing less input from carers. In other words, the value placed on learners through drawing on their memories can have the effect of significantly improving their interest in and engagement with life, and thereby their sense of well-being and active participation in a number of activities far removed from reminiscing.

Most of the examples in this book are drawn from work being done by Norfolk Adult Education's 'Older People's Project', co-ordinated by Margaret Plummer and Jenny Zmroczek, and are therefore based on experiences and projects which have taken place in Norfolk, UK. However, this is not to say that similar work isn't being done or couldn't be done elsewhere, and opportunities for reflection on the ideas presented as well as application to your own setting are provided at the end of each chapter. This book provides a resource of ideas for others to draw on, as well as a guide to good practice in older people's memory work in a learning context. Norfolk Adult Education's 'Older People's Project' is particularly indebted to 'Age Exchange', based in Blackheath, London, for their input in providing training and inspiration to Norfolk's reminiscence tutors.

Note on confidentiality

Throughout the text reference is made to examples of reminiscence work carried out amongst older people and communities in Norfolk. In order to maintain confidentiality, pseudonyms are used and other identifying details changed where participants have either expressed a desire to remain anonymous, or where it was felt that fully informed consent could not be given. In these cases fictional first names, and no surnames are used. All names given to residential homes are pseudonyms.

Chapter 1

Making use of memories in lifelong learning

Making use of memories in lifelong learning

Over the past few years, much has been written and spoken about demographic changes leading to an increasingly ageing population. This, rightly or wrongly, is often perceived as a burden on society, with much concern being expressed about how the country can afford to support its older citizens. In this context, the place of the learning needs of older people takes on a new significance, as it is in the economic interest of society to keep the majority of the population as active and healthy as possible for as long as possible in order to reduce the effects of the perceived burden. The ways in which taking part in learning in general, and working with memories in particular, can benefit older people are the subjects of later chapters, and so will not be fully described here. Instead, the subject of 'making use of memories' is introduced by exploring the backgrounds of lifelong learning, oral history and reminiscence, each of which became popular concepts in the twentieth century.

Lifelong learning

The notion of 'lifelong learning' was first introduced early in the twentieth century. In 1926, Eduard Lindeman described education as a continuing aspect of everyday life arguing that:

- Education is life and the whole of life is learning. Therefore education can have no endings.
- Adult education should be non-vocational – its purpose is to put meaning into the whole of life.
- We should start with situations, not subjects, building the curriculum around the learners' needs and interests.
- We must use the learners' experience: 'The resource of highest value in adult education is the learner's experience' (Lindeman, 1926)

In many ways this book picks up on Lindeman's ideas, looking at practical ways of applying older learners' experiences in an adult education context in the twenty-first century. The form of adult education described by Lindeman in the early part of the twentieth century turns out to be an ideal model for the work being done with older learners in Norfolk today. In the meantime, the concept of lifelong learning has been through various stages, with much emphasis being put on vocational learning and the role of employers and industry in keeping the skills of the workforce up-to-date in a rapidly changing world. While this vocational view of lifelong learning does have a place in the concerns of government, industry and education providers, it has at times been emphasised to the neglect of the needs of older learners who are less likely to need or want to acquire work-related skills.

This book takes a broad view of lifelong learning, seeing it not just as something which can carry on throughout life, but as an important part of living life to the full and maintaining well-being in later life. While in the 1990s the emphasis of lifelong learning was on education being something which should carry on after leaving full-time schooling to ensure a workforce with adequate skills to find and maintain employment in an increasingly competitive job-market, this ignored the full meaning of the term as first conceived. This book demonstrates ways in which learning can truly be lifelong, however long that may be, and whatever changes in ability and living circumstances may take place along the way. Thus, examples are given of learning taking place amongst people with a wide range of abilities and disabilities, in community and residential home settings, with a great deal of emphasis being placed on these learning situations involving a sharing of skills and knowledge between all those who take part, rather than an 'expert teacher' imparting knowledge to 'ignorant students'.

Oral history

It was during the late nineteenth century that historians began to seek first-hand accounts from prominent figures as part of gathering evidence in recording historically significant events. Shortly after Abraham Lincoln's death in 1865, for example, his secretary and law partner began to collect the reminiscences of colleagues who had worked with him. In the decades which followed similar collections were made of the memories of people who had been slaves in the United States, and of general social conditions at the time (Thompson, 2000).

Where manuscripts and printing presses had once brought about a revolution in the range of historical evidence available to the historian, the invention of recording equipment brought along still more changes. The first recording machine was invented in 1877 and by the twentieth century the steel wire recorder was available, with an improved version of this being good enough for use in broadcasting by the 1930s. By the 1940s magnetic tape was available. This is the era when oral history is generally considered to have begun. In the 1960s, much cheaper cassette recorders became available, which moved oral history into the hands of ordinary people. More recent changes in technology have meant that recordings of interviews have become widely available on the Internet, with an unprecedented growth of interest, not only in oral history, but also in its cousins – local history and family history.

The value of oral history lies in the fact that it moves the focus of history from powerful to ordinary people. Instead of an essentially political history, concerned with power-struggles between a few high-ranking figures, and generally being written from the point of view of those who came out on top, oral history opens up new areas of inquiry, looking at what was important to individuals and groups not normally represented in historical accounts, and using the voices of ordinary people without demanding that they have any qualifications other than that they were there and experienced the things of which they speak. Thus the barriers between historians and those they write about are broken down, as well as social barriers, and barriers between generations.

Oral history also widens the scope of history to include emotions and feelings. This enlarges and enriches the scope of historical writing, enabling the reader to become imaginatively involved in what it was like to be there and to live through particular events of the past. It allows the historian to look at things from a number of differing points of view, reflecting the fact that reality is complex and many-sided. It therefore provides a more fully rounded, realistic and fair reconstruction of the past which can be a challenge to the established account. A voice is given to the defeated as well as to the victorious, making oral history essentially more democratic and bringing recognition to groups who have previously been ignored. It is becoming clear that the memories of older people today have an important role in constructing accounts of historically significant events as well as conveying aspects of everyday life which can contribute to an understanding of social history.

Reminiscence

Over the past few decades, reminiscence has come to be seen as a beneficial and potentially therapeutic activity for people of all ages (Bender et al, 1999). Some of the reasons for this are explored in a later chapter, but at this point it is important to note that some of the benefits of reminiscence derive from its similarity to oral history and lifelong learning, in that it *values the experience of the individual.*

Until the 1960s talking about the past was considered to be a sign of withdrawal, degeneration and deterioration in an older person and so was discouraged in health and social care settings. Instead, much emphasis was put on maintaining older people's orientation to present realities, possibly to the detriment of their psychological well-being as they were dissuaded from talking about things which had been important to them throughout their lives. This view began to change in 1963 when Robert Butler published an article on reminiscence and life review pointing out some potential benefits to older people of remembering the past. From that point on, the views of health and social care professionals took a gradual about-turn, until reminiscence was seen as a 'therapy' in the 1980s. Subsequent opinion has taken a step back from this, stating that although reminiscence can have 'therapeutic effects', it is not a 'therapy' as it is not a proven treatment for a particular medical condition (Gibson, 1998: 15).

In the 1980s reminiscence became popular in day centres and residential homes for older people with the publication of Help the Aged's 'Recall' series. Slides were shown together with commentaries on how life used to be, stirring up the memories of older people and stimulating discussion around their own memories, thus enhancing interaction and activity levels (Bornat, 2002b: 2). It is from this movement that the current interest in and practice of reminiscence has drawn inspiration. Reminiscence today consists of a range of social and creative activities undertaken mainly in small groups with the purpose of enhancing the well-being of older learners. The exact nature of how it is undertaken will become clear in subsequent chapters, together with the fact that at the heart of reminiscence activities is the high value placed on individual learners' memories.

Reminiscence and lifelong learning

Here, we use a definition of lifelong learning as a basis for evaluating the part that reminiscence can play in enabling even the most disabled older people to take part in learning activities. Longworth and Davies (1996) give a definition of lifelong learning as:

> the development of human potential through a continuously supportive process which stimulates and empowers individuals to acquire all the knowledge, values, skills and understanding they will require throughout their lifetimes and to apply them with confidence, creativity and enjoyment in all roles, circumstances and environments (Longworth and Davies, 1996: 22)

A cursory glance at this definition indicates immediately that the concept of lifelong learning broadens the horizons of education beyond the requirement of passing exams and gaining qualifications. Learning has relevance for the whole of life. Each part of the definition will be taken and discussed in terms of how this applies to reminiscence as a learning activity for frail older people.

Reminiscence is a useful activity in 'the development of human potential' because it recognises the value of every contribution a learner makes to the group. Older people living in residential homes often feel that they have reached the end of any useful purpose in their lives — a feeling which is not entirely unjustified given the lack of meaningful activities and purposeful roles available to them. Sitting around all day doing nothing can only have a detrimental effect on people's physical, mental and spiritual health. Apathy sets in, taking away the motivation to do something for themselves to make life more fulfilling. Reminiscence provides a way of moving people away from this inactivity, enabling them to discover that they still have the potential to make a valuable contribution within their current environment. Inactivity leads to the deterioration of human potential. An activity like reminiscence can lead

to its growth and development. It is a particularly useful activity with those who have been inactive and need a boost to their confidence. Participation can be progressively graded, so that individuals, who begin by looking at and thinking about items of memorabilia, can move on to making a written or pictorial account of their memories.

Lifelong learning is described as developing human potential through a *'continuously supportive process'*. We shall look both at the 'continuous' and 'supportive' elements in this. 'Continuously' implies that learning opportunities are constantly available. Reminiscence makes this possible by the use of reminiscence rooms, or, where resources are not available for this, reminiscence tables. Learners can use the rooms and tables, and the memorabilia in or on them, to trigger their memories at any time. These can then be shared with friends, staff and visitors, thus making the learning a shared and community process. It is important that such opportunities are continuously available in order to keep up the momentum started in structured group discussions. The more this is the case, the greater the potential of the learning gained through reminiscence to transform the lives of individuals, and with this, the day-to-day atmosphere of the residential home.

Reminiscence can be 'supportive' in that it gives individuals the opportunity to review their personal histories and tackle any unresolved issues from the past. The learning that takes place through this process leaves individuals in a stronger place to deal with current difficulties. This is clearly a lifelong process, and for many people it can be made easier by having the support of a reminiscence group. Support comes from other learners through their listening and through the telling of their own stories as participants gain insight from each other. Having said this, it should be noted that reminiscence is not a form of psychotherapy, and there are limitations to the sort of problems that can be tackled in this way. Reminiscence is also a supportive process in that it does not put pressure on individuals to perform beyond their level of confidence and competence. By listening carefully to the contributions of each learner, the tutor indicates the value of what they are saying and encourages them to go on taking part.

Lifelong learning is described as 'stimulating and empowering individuals'. Learners can gain a sense of control over their past, present and future through the process of reminiscence and life review. Reminiscence can also be seen as giving individuals a voice as the necessary time and space are given to hear what people with communication difficulties have to say. This is something which does not often happen in residential homes as the pressure on carers to get a great number of practical tasks done can sometimes mean that people's mental welfare and individuality is neglected. The reminiscence tutor provides a listening ear which enables people to build up their confidence in communicating despite difficulties. This in turn can lead to them having greater confidence about speaking up in other areas of their lives, thus making it possible for them to make their needs and opinions known. Reminiscence also provides many opportunities for the learners to make choices, as they can choose the extent and the ways in which they take part. People are empowered by being given choices, and as learners become more empowered they can begin to make more decisions about other areas of their lives. This is particularly important within the context of residential care where so many choices can be taken away from individuals for the sake of the smooth running of the home.

Longworth and Davies describe the acquisition of 'knowledge, values, skills and understanding' through lifelong learning. Older people often feel incapacitated in the modern world through their lack of knowledge of such things as computer technologies. The wisdom they have acquired through years of experience can seem inferior to knowledge about fast-moving computers, and one role that reminiscence can have is to reaffirm the importance of such hard-earned wisdom. Through discussion about working life and such things as traditional handicrafts, recognition is given to the skilled craftsmanship practised throughout their lives. At the same time, reminiscence can be used to enable people to develop new skills. As well as expressive skills such as drawing, writing, and drama, computers, recording equipment and cameras can be used. People can work individually or in a group to contribute to archives, local history projects and life history books. In all this, the individual learns more about himself as a person, as well as mastering new skills in communication.

Part of Longworth and Davies' definition of lifelong learning is that it takes place 'throughout life'. The concept of lifelong learning acknowledges the fact that people are able to learn, and have a right to do so, from cradle to grave. Everyone should be given opportunities to learn for as long as they wish to do so, and reminiscence is an activity which can be used for learning at any time of life. It is particularly good at drawing together different age groups, as in intergenerational reminiscence, where young and old can compare and contrast their different ways of doing things.

'Confidence, creativity and enjoyment' are three further elements that are seen as being an integral part of lifelong learning. Equally, they are an integral part of reminiscence, and are amongst the chief motivating factors for those who take part. Many people come to reminiscence groups with very little confidence in their ability to contribute anything, often saying that they just can't remember anything. Older people with cognitive impairments tend to be exposed to a whole battery of 'memory tests' by doctors and psychologists. The effect of this is to emphasise that they are losing their memories, and the low self-esteem and depression this can cause can contribute to the general picture of cognitive decline. Reminiscence puts the emphasis in a completely different place by concentrating on what people *do* remember. This can be a tremendous boost to self-confidence and contributes to the overall enjoyment of the activity. Reminiscence recognises the fact that there are different forms of remembering. While someone may not be able to answer direct questions, they often find that their memories come flooding back when they are exposed to memorabilia and other sensory stimuli.

Longworth and Davies talk about learning being applied in *'all roles, circumstances and environments'*. The process of ageing tends to lead to diminishing roles in our society. At retirement people lose status and responsibilities which may have been the mainstay of their sense of identity. Parenting and grand-parenting roles change as children grow up and physical and mental frailty may reduce the potential for pursuing leisure activities. Roles within the local community tend to be curtailed with the move to residential care. Learning can replace some of these lost roles with new ones. Through reminiscence a person can become not only a 'learner', but also an 'artist', 'writer' or 'historian' as they get involved in recalling and recording their lives in various ways. The confidence this gives them about having a purpose in life can lead to the adoption of more roles within the residential home environment, as they are no longer content to sit back and let life pass them by. This in turn can lead to less dependence on those around them, which can only improve their quality of life.

Having gone this far in describing the role of reminiscence in lifelong learning, there remain some points that need to be made. Firstly, while it is clear that reminiscence can be a useful learning experience in many ways, it is also true that not everybody enjoys it. In fact, some people find it detrimental to their emotional well-being, sometimes because they have traumatic memories which they have not dealt with. Another difficulty is that for reminiscence to be as beneficial as possible, it does need to take place over a long period of time. Unfortunately, most of the funding currently available for reminiscence in residential settings is only short term. Much of this depends on the priorities of residential home managers and their willingness to invest in long-term work. However, there is still little recognition of the rights of older people to take part in lifelong learning activities, and there remains a pervading attitude that people in the Fourth Age have reached the end of their learning potential.

Part of the answer to this problem lies in informing those working with older people about the benefits of lifelong learning and the potential for residents of retirement homes to live purposeful and fulfilling lives. Bringing the concept of lifelong learning into common parlance is something which could transform discriminative attitudes to older people, and change the whole philosophy of care in many residential homes.

In conclusion, it can be said that reminiscence has an important role to play in opening up learning opportunities for frail older people. This is due in part to its adaptability and the fact that it can be extended into many learning activities beyond the initial sharing of memories. One key factor making reminiscence relevant to people of all abilities, and for the entire lifespan, is that it ranges from very simple activities to the more complex. It therefore has a very significant place in providing learning opportunities throughout life

Reminiscence in an educational setting

Questions may be asked at this point as to how reminiscence is used in an educational, as opposed to a social or health context. How can it be seen as learning for an individual to sit and talk about their life experiences? There are a number of answers to this:

- When reminiscence is undertaken in a group, learners use both speaking and listening skills (part of the Core Curriculum for Literacy). This may awaken old skills which had been lost,

develop new skills, or enable learners who have acquired speech, language or hearing impairments to adjust to living with their disabilities.

- Many of the activities undertaken in reminiscence require creativity and self-expression. For some people these will be new skills, for others they will be old skills which are being further developed.
- Reminiscence requires co-operative working, whether through group discussion or in creating a piece of artwork or drama. As well as being a Key Skill and one which could be related to the Citizenship Curriculum, this ability to work alongside others is an essential skill to have in a community living context, such as sheltered housing or a residential home.
- As participants learn about each other's pasts, they gain an understanding of other cultures and alternative experiences to their own. Understanding of historically significant events and social history is likely to be broadened, which is of as much relevance to the study of history as working from a textbook.

A person-centred approach

The basic concern of the humanistic approach in psychology is the human potential for growth. During the 1970s and 1980s this was incorporated into a great deal of theoretical writing about adult education which is relevant to our interest in the value of the experience of the individual in considering the place of memories in lifelong learning. We have already seen how the experiences of individuals are valued in lifelong learning, oral history and reminiscence, and at this point we will relate this to a humanistic perspective on adult learning.

Carl Rogers (1902–1987) was highly enthusiastic about education which engaged with the whole person and with their experiences. He described a number of key elements of learner-centred learning, including the following:

- the teacher needs to trust that the learners are capable of learning;
- the teacher shares the responsibility of the learning process with the students;
- the facilitator provides learning resources and facilitates a learning environment;
- the student develops their own programme of learning and evaluates the extent and significance of their learning. (Rogers, 1977)

Each of these points illuminates the process of sharing memories through oral history and reminiscence in an adult education setting. Learners become fully involved in sharing their own memories and developing their understanding of their experiences and those of others. This can bring about changes in outlook on life and attitudes to self and circumstances by bringing new elements of meaning and understanding into the lives of those who take part. Participation is always voluntary and learners' evaluations of the learning experience can be assessed by their continued and increased participation as well as by verbal and written feedback given to the learning provider. Again, by valuing learners' memories, life experiences can take on new levels of meaning and significance, both in the individual's and group's eyes, as well as within the wider community.

Rogers (1967) also described three core conditions which facilitate learning. The first of these was 'realness in the facilitator of learning'. As the reminiscence tutor shows genuine interest in what the learners have to say, they become increasingly involved and willing to share more memories. Secondly, Rogers advocated 'acceptance'. The reminiscence tutor has an important role in seeing the learner as a person of real value, whatever memories they share. This is linked to the need for realness in the tutor, as they have to take a realistic approach to the fact that nobody is perfect and we can all learn as much from mistakes as from successes in life. The final core condition is 'empathetic understanding' which requires the reminiscence tutor to have a sensitive awareness of how the experience of learning seems to the student, understanding learners from their own point of view and considering the cost to them of sharing their experiences and memories.

Person-centred care in dementia

The person-centred approach has been applied in counselling and care settings as well as to education, and is of significance in our consideration of the place of memories in lifelong learning. Tom Kitwood (e.g. 1997) has advocated the importance of seeing people with dementia as people first. Having dementia is of secondary importance to the way we see individuals, and while it is important to consider the special needs which arise because of the condition, it does not define them as people. Most people with dementia will have significant memory problems, beginning with loss of short-term memory. Memories of the more distant past may stay intact for years after short-term memory begins to deteriorate. Listening to, working with and recording what a person has to say about their life experiences is an essential way of demonstrating their value as a person – both to them and to those around them. By including people with dementia in reminiscence groups, emphasis is placed on what they can still achieve and take part in, rather than on the skills they have lost. This also demonstrates that participation in learning can truly be 'lifelong' and needn't stop at the point of deterioration of cognitive abilities.

Reflection and application

1. What does the term 'lifelong learning' mean to you? How could you broaden its application to people in your locality who are in the later stages of life?
2. At what stage of life, or with what degree of cognitive impairment, do you believe people reach the limits of their learning potential? How could reminiscence activities extend this?
3. Are there people living in your area who could contribute to an oral history collection about such things as a declining industry or the changing nature of inner city living? What would be the benefits of such a collection to the individual participants and the body of knowledge on local social history?
4. Are there minority ethnic or religious communities in your locality who could benefit from sharing their experiences through reminiscence or oral history activities? How can you ensure that both they and the majority population learn from the material produced?

Chapter 2

The benefits of education in retirement

The benefits of education in retirement

Changes in society over the past century have opened up opportunities for learning to a range of socio-economic groups, with university education now being available to a much wider spectrum of people. Research (Sargant et al, 1997) has shown that the better educated you are when young, the more likely it is that you will engage in education in retirement. The implication of this is that because educational opportunities developed throughout the twentieth century, future cohorts of older learners will be keener than the present to take up learning opportunities in later life. This is something to be taken into consideration when planning educational and welfare services for older people.

This chapter focuses on the range and types of benefits older people may gain from taking part in learning, as well as considering what motivates individuals to go back to or continue with learning after the need to gain qualifications for employment has passed. The benefits of education in retirement also extend beyond those applying to the individual, with potential benefits to society resulting from investing in the education of its older members. Some parts of the country, as popular retirement areas, have a higher percentage of older people per head of population, making this a locally relevant topic. However, the proportion of older people is increasing throughout the country, making this of relevance to health and education planners in every area – urban, suburban and rural.

As with all age groups, the most likely people to participate in learning programmes are the affluent and already well educated middle classes. Fewer than one in five of the over-65 age group are involved in current or recent learning, according to a survey carried out by Gallup in 1996 (cited in Carlton and Soulsby, 1999). Many older people are amongst the most socially excluded members of society, especially when compound factors such as class, previous educational experience and disability are taken into consideration. Finishing initial education before the age of sixteen is known to have an adverse effect on the likelihood of participation in learning in later life. This particularly affects women, for whom education was once seen as being of little importance to their primary role as wives, mothers and carers. Until the 1950s it was the norm for women to leave school as soon as they were legally old enough and work only until they got married. As a result many women achieved far less than they were capable of during their initial education, and were less likely to complete work-related training and qualifications at a high level. This has resulted in a large proportion of today's older population having had far less exposure to learning opportunities than subsequent generations.

An ageing population

For the past thirty years, society has invested an enormous amount in the education of younger generations, sometimes seeing older people as obsolete and an economic burden. However, as the 2001 Census shows, around 33.5 per cent of the UK population is aged over fifty, so it doesn't make sense to regard older people in this way. Far from being 'on the scrap-heap', older people represent a rich resource, and it is important that policies and strategies which encourage their continued involvement in all aspects of society are adopted. Involvement in education is one way older people can have their confidence built up, explore new directions for activity and move back into being productive members of society. Use can be made of their extensive life and work experience, at the same time as bringing enjoyment through the social atmosphere of group activities. Learning can be a launch pad and a channel for creative activity, and is essential for maintaining active, independent, healthy lives.

As a society we cannot afford to waste the talents of the increasing number of older people in the population. The cost to society of the disengagement and dependence of a significant proportion of the population are greater, in the long term, than the immediate financial cost of investing in education for older people.

The value of learning

Learning has value for people of any age and every individual has his or her own reasons for becoming involved in education after leaving school. Not only does mastering a new subject or skill provide a great deal of personal fulfilment and raised self-esteem, but taking up learning opportunities also brings the individual into a new social environment in which they can gain confidence and develop social skills. Furthermore, this is usually done in the context of an enjoyable and interesting activity, enhancing motivation and general well-being at the same time as equipping the learner with new knowledge or skills. The skills themselves can be useful in enabling the learner to take a fuller role in society, such as through training for paid or unpaid work and developing caring skills which can be used in family, social or work contexts.

In addition to this general value of learning there are a number of factors to consider which are specific to the needs and experiences of older people. These include:

- The fact that older people have a wealth of experience which can be shared with younger generations, through for example, intergenerational reminiscence or mentoring schemes.
- There is a need to give older people a voice. Their views have often been ignored and discounted in care planning and education provision despite the fact that they are one of the largest potential consumer groups. Older people can be encouraged to speak out and be heard through their involvement in learning experiences.
- Although being older does not inevitably mean being frail or disabled, there is an increasing incidence of disability in later life. Special consideration therefore needs to be given to accessibility and inclusiveness when planning learning programmes for older people.
- Ageism is one of the most widespread forms of discrimination and prejudice in our society, and it inevitably affects the way older people see themselves and the opportunities open to them. A positive effort needs to be made within the education sector to overcome the effects of ageism on individuals and on the planning and structuring of learning programmes.

(Adapted from Carlton and Soulsby, 1999: 11)

The impact of learning on individual lives

A survey by the Institute of Employment Studies (Dench and Regan, 2000) found that 80 per cent of older learners reported a positive impact of learning in at least one of the following areas:

- their enjoyment of life;
- their self confidence;
- how they felt about themselves;
- satisfaction with other areas of their lives;
- their ability to cope with everyday life.

In addition, 42 per cent of learners reported an improvement in their ability to stand up and be heard and their willingness to take responsibility. This has clear implications for older

people's participation in activities which benefit their local communities, and the political arena. This is reflected in the fact that 28 per cent of the older learners questioned also reported increased involvement in either social, voluntary or community activities. In a society which relies more and more, rightly or wrongly, on the involvement of volunteers to maintain the welfare of its most disadvantaged members, such participation is vital to the well-being of local communities, as well as to individuals who would not receive assistance by any other means.

People in poor health also reported benefits from taking part in learning. The IES study found that they were more likely to report that learning improved their enjoyment of life, their self-confidence, their ability to cope, their satisfaction with life and how they felt about themselves, compared to those in better health. (Dench and Regan, 2000: 75)

Some consideration needs to be given to how learning brings about these improvements for people in poor health. Three possible contributory factors are:

1) Providing a new interest

People who become ill or disabled in later life may be inclined to think that their active lives are over, and that it is time to sit back and 'wait to die'. This is particularly the case for those who go to live in residential or nursing homes. Such an attitude increases the likeliness of feelings of depression and hopelessness, as it becomes increasingly difficult to see anything positive in the future. Introducing a new interest at this point can be an effective way of bringing back hope and giving the individual something to get involved in and work on, thus giving a new lease of life.

2) Distraction

Learning has potential for taking lives in new directions, and the interest and involvement in living that this generates in people suffering from poor health can be a distraction from pain and anxiety generated by illness or disability. Research (cited in James, 2001) has shown that one of the best ways of controlling chronic pain is to get involved in activities which distract you from it. For a time, the worry caused by ill health can be forgotten, and it ceases to be the most important thing in life. Learners can begin to identify themselves in terms of something other than their illness – a historian, or an artist (depending on what they are studying) and this frees them up psychologically from the role of a 'disabled person'. Benefits to general well-being follow naturally, as their self-image is restored to that of a 'whole' person.

3) Informing them about their illness

Courses might inform people about specific illnesses or health in general. This has conse-quences for improving well-being, as well as increasing people's confidence in their ability to deal with illness or disability. Individuals who have lost some of their independence through disability may learn new ways of approaching activities of daily living within the boundaries imposed by their impairments.

The economic consequences for the State of such increased well-being in older learners are obvious. As older people maintain their independence for longer, financial savings can be made in terms of fewer carers needing to be employed for fewer hours overall. This further empha-sises the point that the benefits of education in retirement extend far beyond those which apply to the individual, and that money spent on opening up opportunities for learning in later life would be a sound economic investment for any government.

Barriers to learning

The NIACE survey into older learners (1996) found that fewer than one in five older people were involved in current or recent learning. Given such a statistic, it is important to look at what may be deterring older people from returning to learning. Some of the barriers which face older generations include:

- Lack of information, advice and guidance about what is available and how to choose the right course. This is particularly so with changes in the qualifications system which have taken place over the past twenty years. It may be the case that unfamiliarity with current qualifications and the level of study required deters older learners from signing up for courses. The responsibility for this lies with education providers.
- Fear of failure, which may stem from bad school-day experiences. Such fears are perfectly understandable and education providers need to seek ways of overcoming them. One example of providing easily accessible learning is to set up taster classes advertised as being for leisure and pleasure, which give older learners the opportunity to experiment with learning a number of different skills in short sessions without demanding any further commitment to learning. Experience in Norfolk has shown that once older learners have tried courses in the absence of pressure and in an atmosphere which is safe and friendly, they are more likely to sign up for longer courses, sometimes going on to gain qualifica-tions and develop new skills to a high level.
- Location of courses when transport is difficult and costly. Norfolk Adult Education's 'Older People's Project' has tackled this problem by taking learning to the learners. Courses for older learners are run in residential and nursing homes as well as in sheltered housing

schemes, luncheon clubs and other community venues where older people already meet.

- Poor access and facilities for the disabled. This problem is largely overcome by using venues already used by older people. However, sensitivity, awareness and training are needed for tutors providing learning for people who may have multiple physical and sensory disabilities. Activities need to be adapted to suit the needs of individuals, rather than expecting the learners to 'just do the best they can'. Producing results which confirm for learners that they have lost earlier skills seriously detracts from the pleasure of learning. Most activities can be adapted to suit the learners' needs, although this does demand thoughtful and sensitive planning on the part of tutors.

- Cost – funding for older learners is extremely limited and course prices are increasing. In Norfolk this has been partly overcome by training carers working in residential and nursing homes to carry out activities such as reminiscence as part of their everyday work. Funding for this training has come from Social Services. Managers of the 'Older People's Project' have been creative and original in their thinking about applying for funding to provide learning experiences for older people. Funding managers need to think beyond the usual sources of educational funding in order to provide for older learners.

- Attitudes of others about the appropriateness of returning to learning in later life. Some people consider that there is no point in gaining qualifications or developing skills once you reach a certain age or level of disability which is judged to limit your usefulness as a productive member of society. We have already shown that the benefits to the individual and their community make a convincing case for continuing learning at any age.

One of the greatest barriers to learning amongst older people is the view of many that education is for 'other people'. This may have come about as a result of bad school-day experiences, and the lack of encouragement or opportunity to explore education as an adult. This is particularly so for those who are from the lower socio-economic groups and have spent their lives in jobs requiring little skill, and offering little status or pay. Some older women are affected by the view that they should continually sacrifice their own fulfilment to the needs and expectations of others. This has traditionally been part of the role of wife and mother, and is difficult to shift in a society which still expects women to be 'natural carers'. Other people may be socially isolated, and rather than this spurring them on to get involved in learning, it compounds their lack of self-esteem and confidence, making it even more difficult for them to try out new social situations.

The development of education provision over recent years has not supported older people's learning. In particular, older people have been restricted as a consequence of the Further and Higher Education Act 1992, which directed resources towards academic and vocational courses at the expense of learning for its own sake. More recently, providers have been put under pressure through allocation of resources to give priority to 14–19-year-olds. As a result adult education providers have tended to narrow the range of the curriculum, increase course fees and reduce fee-remissions for the over-60s.

What motivates older people to learn?

A group of twenty retired learners in Norfolk were asked by the author to rate a list of reasons for engaging in learning in order of their importance. They were also interviewed about their experience of learning, motivation to study and any barriers they have faced. Information gathered from the interviews and questionnaires only gave insight into the motivation and experience of these particular people as it was not a large enough sample to warrant generalisations to a wider group. However, through this research it was possible to get a clearer picture of some of the factors which attract older people to learning, what benefits they gain from it and some of the difficulties they face.

Participants were asked to put a tick next to items that applied to them either strongly or fairly strongly on a list of possible reasons for taking part in adult education classes. The results, placed in order of the number of times each item was ticked by learners, are shown in Table 1.

Table 1: Reasons for taking part in adult education
(20 retired learners in Norfolk)

	Total ticks
1) Keeping my mind active keeps it healthy	14
2) I want to take part in a meaningful activity	13
3) It is part of a hobby/ I am pursuing an interest	13
4) I want to meet people and socialise	12
5) It satisfies my search for understanding or knowledge	12
6) It gives meaning to my life	11
7) I am learning particular skills for a specific purpose	9
8) It is building my confidence or self-esteem	9
9) It gets me out of the house	3
10) It fills my time	2

Each one of the ten items was ticked by some of the participants, highlighting the difficulty of drawing meaningful conclusions applicable to a wider group from this small sample. What the data do tell us is that this group of older people had a wide range of reasons for undertaking learning and that a wider sample is likely to have confirmed this heterogeneity. It is also reasonable to assume that there are many reasons for wanting to learn in later life which were not included on the list and which would apply to some individuals.

Looking at the three items which were given the most importance by the twenty learners, it is possible to draw out some ideas which might be important in a teaching situation. Firstly, the item of most overall importance was 'keeping my mind active keeps it healthy'. This implies that these older learners wanted intellectual stimulation that was going to give them some challenges, and that thought provoking material would be appropriate for them. Secondly, the next two items suggest that they want that material to be meaningful and relevant to their interests. This points towards the sorts of services education, health and social care providers need to be delivering. There is a strong need in each of us for challenge, interest and variety in the activities we undertake whatever our age. This highlights the importance of involving older people in planning their learning by asking them how they'd like to learn as well as what they'd like to learn.

The items on the questionnaire which were considered least important by the participants were 'it fills my time' and 'it gets me out of the house'. This indicates that these learners wanted more than time-filling entertainment and that there was something about the learning situation and its challenges which attracted and motivated them. They wanted to use and develop their intellect and skills.

During the follow-up interviews all participants emphasised the pleasure they got from meeting people and socialising, and had found that doing courses offered a relaxing and interesting way to do so, partly because there was an assumption that they would already have something in common with people who signed up for the same course. Some participants benefited particularly from the mental stimulation and enjoyed the freedom that retirement gave them to pursue subjects for interest rather than because they had to. Others saw education as a way of opening up more opportunities in the future, by for example, maintaining physical and mental well-being so that they could go on holiday.

One participant began her course soon after bereavement, at a time when she was looking for ways to meet new people. In a similar vein, others had been invited to join reminiscence and art groups by social workers involved in their care. In each of these cases being involved in learning has brought improvements to the mental health of participants, and one lady had regained more physical mobility than doctors had expected after an illness. While it is unwise to conclude from these examples that learning is the cure for all ills, it is certainly the case that the participants themselves see their involvement in their courses as a significant factor in maintaining the will to remain independent and overcome adverse life events.

Barriers to learning

These older learners were concerned about the lack of awareness amongst tutors about hearing loss in later life, and felt that their needs were sometimes ignored or misunderstood when they were unable to hear.

All participants said that they had been put off doing courses by the fact that so many of them are now accredited, and some had experience of being charged extra not to work towards a qualification on an accredited course. They all felt that having worked hard all their lives, they wanted to be able to pursue their interests for pleasure, without being put under pressure to have assignments in on time.

Case study

Brenda was one of six children and had a happy early childhood, with a close relationship to her father. At the age of 10 she fell down stairs and was left unable to walk unaided until the age of 15. This was extremely disruptive to her education. On the whole she was taught at home, but went back to school for six weeks when she was 13. This brief return to school ended after the teacher disciplined her for talking by making her stand in the corner for an hour. This caused her immense pain and from then on she refused to go to school.

Brenda was able to find work at the age of 14 through a friend of her father's. At the outbreak of war in 1939, she was working in hotel catering. The hotel building was taken over by the War Office and she was made redundant. From there, she went to work in a food factory, where she eventually became supervisor.

Brenda met her husband during the war. They got married when he was on 24 hour embarkation leave, and after that she didn't see him for five years as he was taken prisoner. When he finally returned home he was in poor health and needed nursing. They eventually bought a butcher's shop where they worked together. Brenda had three children, but only one daughter survived.

Five years ago she had a serious fall and broke her pelvis and leg. She required a major operation and was told that she would not walk again and was likely to be doubly incontinent. She refused to accept either of these things and saw overcoming these problems as a challenge. She was discharged from hospital after six weeks and for the first 18 months after the accident felt extremely isolated. She could not go out because her husband also had disabilities and could not push a wheelchair. Friends who called in the early weeks gradually stopped doing so. She describes herself as having become increasingly lonely, depressed and 'brain-dead'. As a result she was visited by a social worker, who referred her to a reminiscence group.

On first walking into the reminiscence room her spirits lifted. She had felt very nervous about going, but the atmosphere in the room (set out in the style of a 1940s living room) immediately brought back memories. At the group she has found purpose and meaning for her life in sharing her memories and listening to those of other people. She likes to look out for the needs of others, and the group provides a context in which she can do this. She feels that her mind has come to life again and she has regained her social confidence. Although an emotionally expressive woman, she is no longer depressed, and enjoys having fixed points in her week to look forward to. She now takes part in an art class for older people as well as reminiscence, and finds that this interest in art gives her something to talk about with other people

Brenda has gradually increased her mobility to the point of being able to move around indoors with two walking sticks, and has recovered from her depression by making the most of her weekly reminiscence experience and art classes.

Conclusion

Education in retirement has many benefits for those who take part and this is indicative of the beneficial role of learning across all age-groups. However, apart from the ways in which individuals gain, there are also benefits for society in general. Lifelong learning has an important role to play in enabling older people to maintain and develop healthy independent lives. Learning can enable older people to lead more fulfilling lives as active citizens in their community, contributing to the well-being of others by being involved in voluntary work and by sharing the wealth of their experience and knowledge. Given these clear benefits, it is essential that more is done to open up learning opportunities to the older generation, breaking down the barriers to learning which exist both within individuals and within society.

Reflection and application

1. How do the benefits of education in retirement compare with those experienced by younger generations?
2. Suggest ways in which learning experiences might equip and enable older people to become more involved in their local communities. How could this benefit your community?
3. How can you or your organisation work with older learners to reduce and remove barriers to learning?

Chapter 3

The benefits of reminiscence

The benefits of reminiscence

In the last chapter we considered the value that education in general can have for older people and concluded that the benefits were many and varied. This chapter focuses on the specific benefits which can be experienced through reminiscing. Although reminiscence is usually associated with older people, people of any age can and do take part in it. The primary school child writing an essay about what he or she did in their summer holiday is reminiscing, as are the 40-year-olds at their school reunion discussing their former teachers and classmates. In fact, most of us do some reminiscing every day as we look back and reflect on how our lives are progressing or at what we have achieved through a particular piece of work. Reminiscence is an ordinary human activity which we participate in throughout our lives.

While reminiscing is not an activity restricted to older people, it can have particular value when introduced as a structured activity in later life. This is largely because it is a holistic and person-centred approach, respecting and valuing the memories of individuals at the same time as developing relationships within groups and enabling people to extend their social networks. Some of the purposes and benefits of reminiscence are explored below. Together they indicate how this approach can meet the needs of the whole person.

Encouraging sociability

As group members talk together about their lives and experiences in reminiscence sessions, they often discover common ground and through this develop new relationships. They may have lived near each other as children, worked in similar jobs or had similar experiences of family life. Many older people suffer from social isolation and loneliness as a result of losing touch with friends after finishing work, moving home or through bereavement. With their level of activity being reduced after retirement they may not have the same opportunities to make new friends as in the past. Within a reminiscence group, whilst listening to the stories shared, participants find that their interest in each other grows and they begin to establish deeper levels of communication through asking questions and being able to relate to one another. This is particularly the case in residential and nursing homes where the once familiar picture of a group of older residents sitting next to the same people all day every day and not even knowing their names is being broken down through the introduction of activities such as reminiscence.

Case studies

Ilene and Leonard had been attending the same day centre for two months before they realised that they were cousins. They had lost contact with each other as children after a family rift, and it was only through talking about their families in a reminiscence session that each realised who the other was. They now spend a great deal of time talking with each other and catching up on all that has happened in the intervening years.

Martin had moved to a residential home after spending months in a psychiatric hospital with depression. The move to residential care was hard for him as it meant the end of his hope of ever living independently again. This had deepened his depression from the time of his arrival and he found it hard to interact with other residents. After living at the home for a month he was persuaded by the activity co-ordinator to try out the reminiscence group. He did not take an active role in the group the first time he attended, but sat and listened to the other residents. In subsequent weeks he had no hesitation about joining the group, but still limited his participation to listening to others. Some weeks later the topic under discussion was 'working lives' and each group member talked about the work they had undertaken before retirement. It was at this point that Martin discovered that another resident had worked in the same factory as him. Although the two men had not known each other at that time they talked at some length about their work and from that day on Martin became far more active and sociable both in the reminiscence group and around the home.

Encouraging feelings of self-worth and confidence

As well as enabling group members to find common ground, reminiscence can confirm a sense of unique identity. Each person is different, and this individuality of experience and personality can be expressed through the telling of life-stories. Individuals reveal themselves to the group not only through recounting what they have done during their lives, but also in the way they tell their stories. Attitudes and feelings are just as important as where someone was and what they did, and the experience of being listened to builds story-tellers' confidence in the significance of their story, as well as in their ability to express themselves and take part in group activities. Furthermore, the older person is the expert on his or her own past, so this is an area in which the story-teller can have confidence that he or she knows more than the audience. Given that the experience of many people living in residential and nursing homes is of dependency and helplessness, it can give a remarkable boost to self-esteem to be the person who has something interesting and unique to say – something to give which is valued by the listener.

Case study

Ivy was a very quiet lady who listened to other people's stories in the reminiscence group but did not contribute her own until the tutor approached her individually and asked her where she had spent her childhood. Ivy was very dismissive of her own experience and as she spoke about her life her body language and tone of voice suggested that it was of little significance and not really worth talking about. It happened that Ivy had been brought up in the same village in the Fens as the reminiscence tutor's parents, thus eliciting particular interest on her part. When Ivy realised that the tutor was listening eagerly to her description of the farm on which she lived, the tone of her voice changed and she became more animated. Although it was necessary for the tutor to continue giving Ivy individual attention and encouragement in subsequent sessions, care staff noticed that she began to talk more openly during everyday activities, and this helped them to see her as a more interesting person with whom they enjoyed spending time.

Restoring a sense of identity

Self image can be seriously affected by the ageing process, in regard to both physical appearance and cognitive ability. The physical changes that take place in our bodies throughout our lives can be both surprising and disturbing, and even at the age of forty, the person we see looking back at us from the mirror each morning might not be quite as young as the person we expect to see. This can be even more so for people in later life as they may feel much younger at heart than their body tells them they are. Equally, brain cells begin to die off from our twenties onwards. By the time we reach retirement age this can result in slower thinking and some difficulties with memory. This benign senescent forgetfulness is quite different from the changes that occur in dementia, but can lead to concern for some people that it is a sign of a failing mind.

With all these changes to the individual, together with changes in occupation, housing, relationships and financial status, it can become difficult for older people to maintain a sense of their own identity. Reminiscing can help with this process through reaffirming that someone is still the same person who held down a job for forty years, nursed children, travelled, played a musical instrument, sang in the church choir or 'dug for victory'. Inwardly, the person is unchanged, with the same value, and so can have the same level of self-esteem associated with his lifetime's achievements. The whole of a person's past has contributed to who he or she is today, and reviewing life in the context of reminiscence can help a person come to terms with changed circumstances and diminished roles. It also gives the individual a new role as a story-teller and historian, thereby lessening the tendency to fall into the role of 'helpless patient'. The more an individual sees him- or herself as having significant roles, and the stronger their sense of identity, the less likely it is that they will be treated by others as insignificant or helpless. The overall quality of a person's life and psycho-social environment will thereby be improved, enhancing general well-being.

Case study

Greenfields Nursing Home introduced the practice of using a reminiscence group as a way of gathering information about their residents to contribute to care plans. With the knowledge of the residents, the reminiscence tutor worked together with the activity co-ordinator and care staff to compile information about the past lives and achievements of group members. This was found to be particularly useful with new residents, who sometimes arrived with no information other than their medical history and medications. It became possible to affirm each resident's sense of identity through discussions about the past during routine care activities as well as planning activity programmes around their expressed and established interests. This changed the nature of care relationships as the older people were seen to have experiences of interest and relevance to the younger carers. Residents were no longer talked about in terms of their deficits, but instead were viewed as whole people with a wealth of experience and many remaining strengths.

Passing on family history and cultural heritage

Reminiscence is a way of passing on knowledge and understanding of the past to younger generations, and as such has value not only for the reminiscers, but also for those listening to their recollections, including the wider community. A distinction is sometimes drawn between reminiscence and oral history by saying that reminiscence is for the benefit of the reminiscer while oral history is for the benefit of the listener (for extended discussions comparing reminiscence with oral history see Gibson, 2004: 38–41 and Bornat, 2002a). However, there is a great deal of overlap between the two. Much of the value of reminiscence lies in the fact that ordinary people's voices are heard on ordinary topics. Few academic historians worry themselves with how working-class women did their housework in the early part of the twentieth century, but this is the kind of material that is of great significance in reminiscence as it brings back memories of everyday life, and with it, the memory of the people with whom that life was lived. Reminiscence brings the past to life, adding interest to a subject which can seem rather dry if experienced only through textbooks. It can also play a significant role in bringing to life characters from the past as relationships with family, friends and neighbours are described.

Case study

Andrew had never known his extended family as his mother died when he was young and he and his sisters moved away from Cornwall when their father's promotion at work led to a move to the London area. They had not kept in touch with his mother's side of the family and he had little knowledge of his family history on either side as his father didn't talk about his own family or the past. Throughout his childhood and early adult life Andrew felt that it was impossible to have a relationship with his father as his only interest was work, and conversation between them was always stilted. After retiring, his father began taking adult education classes aimed at the over-60s. One of these was on local and family history and involved him doing a project of his own choosing at the end of the course. He chose to write about his own childhood together with doing some family history research. When he had completed it he sent a copy to Andrew who was thrilled by what he read. For the first time he was able to see his father as a whole person, and became intrigued by the characters his father described – his own relatives. Andrew's relationship with his father improved from then on, to the point of their taking a holiday together in Cornwall in order to carry out more research.

Meeting the needs of the whole person

Taking part in a reminiscence group can meet the needs of the whole person as activities can be designed to include emotional, intellectual, spiritual, creative, social and physical aspects. Some of these aspects will be explored further in later chapters. Activities can be adapted by the skilled reminiscence tutor to suit the abilities of individuals, with the pace and degree of stimulation varied in accordance with the needs of group members.

Psychologists have suggested that the main reason the human brain is so large in proportion to our bodies is that we need this extra capacity in order to develop skills of language, co-operation and sociability to live together in communities. One of the needs of human beings, therefore, is to live in relationship with a variety of other people, and it can be problematic when groups of older people, such as those living in nursing and residential homes, become separated from the rest of the community. Through reminiscence, older people can become involved in intergenerational work and community learning projects, thus reducing this exclusion. This will be explored further in later chapters.

A word of caution

Despite the wide range of benefits that can be gained from reminiscence, it is not an activity which suits everyone (Coleman, 1993: 106). Some people are not interested in talking about the past, and others find it too upsetting to think about and don't want to be reminded. Individual choice should be respected at all times and assumptions about older people enjoying talking about the past should never be made. Offer the invitation and opportunity to join in, and then respect the choice that is made, always being open to a change of mind in the future.

Case study

Reminiscence in a residential home for older people

Sunrise is a privately owned residential home for older people, and is home to twenty-four people who are unable to live independently for reasons of mental and physical disability. In January 2005 the home manager reviewed the existing activities programme in the light of Standard Eight of the Department of Health's 'National Service Framework for Older People' which suggests that support should be given to enable 'older people to live lives which are as fulfilling as possible'. Realising that existing activities were unsatisfactory the manager contacted the local adult education department who provided a series of eight reminiscence sessions

The eight sessions were planned to cover themes which are likely to be of interest to and include the experiences of most older people such as schooldays, household tasks and working life. One of the principal aims of the first session was to create a psychologically safe environment for group members to talk about anything which interested them. This was done through using non-threatening warm-up activities to indicate to residents that they could contribute as much or as little as they wished. Pressure was never put on anyone to take part in anything they felt uncomfortable with.

Each session had a similar structure with the warm-up activity being followed by discussion, looking at and handling memorabilia, and quizzes. On most occasions there was also the opportunity to take part in a creative activity, such as writing or drawing.

Outcomes

From the first session it was clear that participation in the reminiscence group was going to have a beneficial effect for many of the residents. Specific benefits which were reported at the end of the eight sessions were as follows:

- *The general level of social interaction within the home increased, with one resident who tended to stay in her room much of the time deciding to come out and join the sessions, and subsequently interacting more with other residents and care staff.*
- *One resident who up until then had only spoken in monosyllables since moving to Sunrise, began to take part in discussions with the reminiscence tutor and care staff. He clearly benefited from their willingness to listen and felt that his individual life experiences were valued and important. Other residents later began to include him more in conversations.*
- *Visitors commented on the increased level of communication of their friends and relatives, and the subsequent increase in their own enjoyment of visits. Residents talked about the reminiscence sessions with their visitors who then wanted to find out more about the residents' lives by asking questions.*
- *Care staff benefited from the reminiscence programme as they came to see the residents as whole people who had an identity and a life story apart from their present situation and need for care. This had a marked effect on the quality of care given, as staff now engage residents in conversation about their lives during routine care activities:*
  Ralph is no longer the 'ninety-year-old with dementia', but is respected for and talked with about his forty years experience as a farmer;

Molly is no longer the 'sullen lady with the stroke', but is seen as having a subtle sense of humour as she relates her experiences working in a munitions factory during the war. Other residents have gained respect and enhanced self-identity as they have passed round family snapshots and some of the items of their own memorabilia which they have brought with them to Sunrise. This new view of residents has contributed to staff gaining greater satisfaction from their work.

At the end of the eight sessions all the residents who had taken part said that they had enjoyed them and would like more. This was relayed to the home owner who arranged for the sessions to continue.

Reflection and application

1. How might reminiscence and related activities benefit older people you know? Include those living in their own homes, as well as those in residential, nursing and day care settings.
2. How would it alter your perspective on older people if you knew about their past achievements and interests? How might a change in your approach enhance their quality of life and your enjoyment of your work?
3. How much do you know about life in a residential home? Find out about the residential, nursing and day care facilities in your area and ask if you can go in to talk to the clients about their past and present experiences. How does this alter or challenge your perspective on the later stages of life?
4. What opportunities exist in your local area for using reminiscence as a means of widening participation in education by involving older learners?
5. What resources might you need to draw on to make this possible? What skills do you and your colleagues already have which could facilitate this and how could you equip yourselves to get more involved in reminiscence activities?

Chapter 4

Memories –
a great learning
resource

Memories – a great learning resource

Without memory we could not benefit from past experience, and therefore could not learn anything. Memory is essential throughout life as we learn to adapt to our social environments and relate to other people, in learning skills which enable us to earn a living and in functioning in everyday life through personal care and organising our homes. Without the ability to remember, a child could not learn to recognise his own parents, tie his shoelaces or feed himself. As adults we could not learn to cook, drive or even make a cup of tea. Memory is essential to our survival as individuals and to our progress as a society.

The study of memory featured prominently in the early days of psychology as a science, yet having been studied in a sustained way for over 50 years, it is still surrounded by much mystery. Many different theories have been put forward as to how memories are laid down and retrieved, with memory being described at different times as a filing system, a series of computer circuits and as chemical changes to brain cells. What does seem fairly clear is that there are different types of memory and that the word 'memory' refers to three distinct processes, namely registration, storage and retrieval. *Registration* refers to the information which goes into the memory system. While it is a necessary condition for storage to take place, it is not in itself a sufficient condition. Not everything which registers on the sensory receptors will be stored because, for example, of selective attention and the fact that our brains would become overloaded if we remembered everything we perceive. *Storage* refers to the process by which sensory information is retained in memory and can be seen as a necessary, but not a sufficient, condition for *retrieval*. That is, you can only remember something which has been stored, but the fact that it has been stored is no guarantee that you will be able to recall it on any particular occasion. Many people have the experience of walking out of an examination room and then remembering the answer to a question which they had spent too much time struggling over and not resolving under exam conditions. For information held in storage to be retrieved the conditions have to be right, and there are a number of different ways in which recall can be assisted. These include using sensory triggers such as music, aromas and visual cues which remind us of the occasion on which we last experienced these triggers. Hence, a woman in her seventies who thought she had forgotten all about a young man she had had a relationship with fifty years earlier, suddenly had a vivid picture of him in her mind when she heard the song 'A nightingale sang in Berkeley Square'. Not only did she remember what he looked like, but also the things he said, the circumstances of their parting and the sensation of his touch. Such experiences can seem quite overwhelming to some people, not necessarily because of the nature of the memories, but more because of the strength with which they can come flooding back when the right triggers are used.

Another way of enhancing recall in older people is to hold reminiscence sessions in 'reminiscence rooms'. These are rooms set out with the furnishings and décor of a bygone era, for example a kitchen or living room decorated in 1940s style. Activities held in these rooms often enhance the level of functioning of older people with dementia as they relax in this environment and fall into a way of being, which is more familiar to them than the equipment and pace of modern life. Psychological research has shown that recall can be improved by the external cues of the environment – this is why police use reconstruction of crime scenes in an attempt to prompt the memories of potential witnesses, and also why it can be easier to do an examination in the room where learning originally took place rather than in unfamiliar surroundings.

Case study

Sheila Hawkes, a reminiscence tutor working with Norfolk Adult Education's 'Older People's Project', is also the Deputy Manager of a residential care home for older people. With the assistance of residents at the home, Sheila set up a 1940s kitchen and a 1950s lounge.

The whole project was owned by the residents from start to finish since they became motivated as much by the process of creating the rooms as looking forward to the finished product. Sheila brought in a sink for which a male resident made a wooden frame while a female resident sewed curtains to go round it. Several residents were involved in helping with these tasks as well as through asking family and friends for furnishings and other items with which to fill the rooms. Word spread amongst the residents as one enthused another, and in time involved their family and friends. The whole project took several months to complete and in many ways the actual creation of the rooms was as beneficial to the residents as the reminiscence sessions later held in them.

During the construction, residents worked on their tasks and motivated each other without the assistance of staff being necessary, whereas once the rooms were in use a member of staff needed to be present to encourage structured reminiscing. It was found that the kitchen was best for one-to-one work with people with dementia, while the lounge worked well for reminiscence groups. The project as a whole was successful because it was something that residents could get thoroughly involved in and own for themselves.

As well as the processes of registration, storage and retrieval, memories can be seen as being laid down in three different stages. Again, the first of these stages involves the perception of events and sensations through the sensory receptors. For example, in learning the telephone number of a friend you intend to call you quickly look at and say under your breath the series of numbers. You have created a *sensory memory*. You then repeat the number to yourself in order to create a *short-term memory*. If you dial the number straight away and do not use it again for some time, the memory is likely to be lost. However, if you rehearse the number over and over again by frequent reminders, repetition and use, the number is likely to become fixed in *long-term memory*. I have used many hundreds of telephone numbers during the course of my life, most of which have been forgotten as soon as they have been dialled, many of which I still have to look up every time I want to use them. And yet there are some numbers which I used frequently as a child but have not used at all for the past 25 years, such as the phone numbers of school friends, which I can still recall with no apparent effort. Psychologists believe that long-term memories are associated with permanent structural changes in nerve cells and are remarkably resistant to destruction. Sensory and short-term memory, on the other hand, may only involve temporary chemical and electrical changes to the cells. This is one reason why, as damage to nerve cells occurs in conditions like dementia, it is the long-term memories which are most enduring.

As well as the different processes involved in remembering, and the three stages of laying down memories, there are different *types* of memory – *procedural and declarative*. Declarative memory is associated with being able to recite facts, and so is very useful in passing exams and remembering what you need from the shops. It answers the 'what', 'where' and 'when' questions, for example:

- What sort of car have you got?
- Where did you buy your car?
- When did you last have your car serviced?

Learning to drive a car starts off as a declarative memory as you listen to the instructor's explanation and then talk yourself through the sequence of movements as you carry them out. However, in time you know these movements so well that you can do them without even thinking about them. Driving a car has now become part of procedural memory. In the process the memory has been converted from being quite fragile to something quite resistant to destruction. The process of frequent repetition has converted a declarative memory into a procedural one. Procedural memory answers the question:

- How do you drive a car?

The difference here, compared with the 'what', 'where' and 'when' questions of declarative memory, is that while it is easy to drive a car once you have learned, it is very difficult to explain the process to other people. The memory exists in the movement pattern of your muscles rather than as a list of instructions. This is why people need extensive training in order to learn to be driving instructors. Anyone who has tried to give their child driving lessons will know that it is not enough to be able to drive a car to know how to teach other people to do so! Likewise, the best drivers are not necessarily the best instructors, just as the

most talented pianists are not necessarily the best music teachers. While procedural memory comes out of declarative memory it is much more difficult to reverse the process and explain the component parts once you have acquired a skill.

In people with dementia, the procedural skills are often the last to go. This is why *Alice*, a lady in her late eighties who had Alzheimer's disease, was still able to play the piano beautifully at the music group she attended, even though when asked she always said she could not play. When seated in front of the piano she would at first look at it having no idea what to do, but if encouraged to place her fingers on the keys, within seconds she would be playing beautifully and leading the whole group in singing. This gave her self-esteem a great boost and created a feeling of well-being which lasted long after the end of the group, even though she would forget within minutes of stopping that she could play at all. This is a process which has been observed amongst many older people with dementia. Indeed, some people who hardly speak at all, and who have very few retrievable memories, can often sing several verses of familiar hymns or recite whole poems, which they learnt by heart and practised frequently as children.

Case study

Janice was a quiet member of a reminiscence group, who rarely contributed anything to discussions. The reminiscence tutor was aware that she had been brought up on a dairy farm and so looked for items which might trigger her memories of this. One day, Janice was handed some butter pats. She immediately picked them up and began miming shaping blocks of butter. At the same time she began to speak, describing what hard work it had been churning the butter, how it had to be done at just the right speed and temperature, and how lovely butter had tasted in those days. Other group members agreed, sharing their experiences of seeing butter pats used in shops and describing the taste of butter in the past. Janice went on to describe the farm where she had lived, and some of the dairymen who had worked there. The key to Janice's memories had been in the movement of using the butter pats, which was related to her procedural memory, rather than in just looking at them.

Memories and the affirmation of identity

In looking at the importance of memories one thing to consider is how recounting memories relates to self-identity and how we come to have a self-image in the first place. Michael Argyle (1983: 196–7) describes a number of elements which make up our self-image, including adolescent identity, social roles, and the reactions of others. In considering these points, we shall look at how telling our story through reminiscence and oral history is related to and reinforces our self-image and sense of identity.

The late teens and early twenties have been identified as the time of life when self-identity is being established away from parental expectations. Daniel Levinson's model of the 'Seasons of a man's life' (1978) describes an Early Adult Transition from the ages of 18 to 22 which involves increasing moves towards all kinds of independence and exploration of life's possibilities such as occupational choice and personal identity. Erik Erikson (e.g. 1980) also describes the psychosocial crisis for the teen years as being 'Identity v. role confusion'. Argyle describes this period as an important time for acquiring self-identity:

Somewhere between the ages of 16 and 24 there is often an identity crisis, when a person is forced to make up his mind about which... pieces of identity to hang on to and which to suppress (Argyle, 1983: 198).

This time of life can be seen as particularly important in terms of reminiscence. Rubin et al, (1986, cited by Coleman, in Bornat, 2002a: 13) describe how graphs which record the ability of older people to recall events from their past show a noticeable bump in the line of the graphs indicating enhanced recall of memories from the period of roughly 15–30 years of age. This backs up the anecdotal evidence of reminiscence tutors who have sometimes noted that the most lively reminiscence groups are those which focus on events during the late teens and early twenties such as leaving school, starting work and getting married.

Every change that occurs in the life course is a potential threat to a person's sense of identity and therefore requires adjustment. Old age could be seen as having particular significance in this regard, in that it is more likely that the changes are unwanted and that many occur together over a short time-span. These include such things as loss of work role, loss of spouse, decreased income and increased physical frailty. These changes are not always prepared for and there is little time for adjustment between each. Associated with this rapid rate of change can be loss of meaningful roles which Gutmann (cited by Coleman, in Bornat, 2002a: 19) sees as leading to many of the pathological features associated with old age in western society (e.g. depression, anxiety, mental deterioration, etc). Coleman (1993: 105) describes 'Identity maintenance' theory, suggesting that a greater identification with past lives and past achievements is helpful to older people in situations of deprivation and loss. The discrepancy between how one would like to live one's life and how one is actually living it is minimised by stressing the value of the life that has already been lived, which in itself justifies a sense of self-worth. There can also be a connection between what has been achieved in the past and what the older person is facing now, such as triumph in the face of adversity. Older people, through remembering how they have coped in the past can learn from this how to adapt to and cope with the present.

In a study of veterans of the Spanish–American War McMahon and Rudick (1964, cited by Coleman, in Bond et al (eds), 1993: 105) found that reminiscence seemed closely related to freedom from depression. The reminiscence of these men was of a story-telling nature and tended to exaggerate the value of the past in comparison to the present. McMahon and Rudick suggested that reminiscence had a significant part to play in the context of loss of role and function in old age, in preserving self-respect by investing in and stressing the importance of the image of oneself as one has been. By identifying past accomplishments, the gap is narrowed between a present concept of self characterised by role loss and the ideal self informed by the concept of intrinsic human worth, regardless of role and economic or social position.

If one of the defining features of ageing is loss, this loss is exaggerated in dementia which deprives people of attributes which contribute to a sense of security – a continuous identity, memories of person and place, and powers of reasoning. Interviews carried out by reminiscence tutors for Norfolk Adult Education's 'Older People's Project' provided evidence of some people with dementia holding on to their identity as 'people who survived the war or fought for their country'. One man, who has poor short-term memory and has lost his conversational skills, pointed repeatedly to the tattoos on his arm which listed the places he served as a soldier in the Second World War, asking the reminiscence tutor to read them to him. He carried written on his body the memories which were most important to him. Other people, when asked to draw pictures of themselves as part of a creative reminiscence group, drew themselves in service uniforms. Though it may be argued by some that we should encourage older people to live in the present, the realities of this may be too painful or confusing by comparison with the achievements, sense of identity and stronger self-image of the past. It is therefore clear that recounting experiences from the past can lead to greater happiness and well-being for some people than struggling to make sense of day-to-day life in the present.

Symbolic Interactionists are interested in how people define their own circumstances and identities, and labelling theory is a particular application of this approach. One of the important features of labelling is the effect it has on both the person being labelled and other people around them. Receiving a diagnostic label, for instance, is likely to affect the way individuals behave with others as they may act the role the new label implies, partly in response to the way others act towards them. One of the difficulties facing older people is that in being labelled 'the elderly' they are somehow seen as being a homogenous group in society who are past their best and have little left to contribute. Reminiscence frees people from such labels by emphasising what individuals have achieved, and are still achieving, and by valuing their unique memories.

Many people when taking part in reminiscence groups or contributing to oral history recordings are talking for the first time about traumatic experiences they have had. This may be due in part to the lack of counselling in the past, as well as the fact that some people felt it was wrong to talk about their suffering when others had suffered as much, if not more. It is likely that these people who have kept quiet about their experiences have had their lives seriously affected by the burden of carrying around memories which they either felt they could not talk about or that others wouldn't want to know. Their experiences have had a marked effect on how they see themselves – but this has remained largely a hidden part of their identities. By talking about the experiences through reminiscence, they have been able to stand up and reveal a part of their inner selves, and so find peace from the burden of their memories.

A story is not just about what happened, but is also an interpretation, a way of explaining to others, and to yourself, the meaning of those events. Life stories are social constructions presented from the point of view of the teller. By telling their stories older people are able to construct a meaning for events, and therefore come to a new understanding of their role with each new telling. Hence the same events are described with a new emphasis each time, while the crucial factors remain the same. One man recounted his experience of the D-Day landings, but each time he repeated his story, something new was introduced. He was creating meaning for himself by telling and re-telling the story.

The losses and changes experienced in later life all have consequences for maintaining social networks. Our ability to make ourselves more interesting to other people at this point in our lives may ensure continuing relationships in the present and the future. In seeking meaning for one's own life, most people find it necessary to locate themselves within a wider collective or larger framework. The Depression of the 1930s was a time when everyone was under similar kinds of pressure and there can be a strong sense of communal identity amongst groups of people talking about their experiences at this time. Similarly people who lived through the Second World War, worked in similar trades and industries, or lived in the same towns, villages or suburbs, can find points of common identity as they share their memories. Although we try to develop a coherent story that gives shape to our lives, this is more readily achieved if we can locate ourselves within a broader framework in which we are assured

of being connected to or in relationships with other people. Being part of a reminiscence group where others are sharing similar stories can provide that broader framework, hence a readiness on the part of some older people to talk at length in these groups about experiences which they have kept to themselves up until that point.

Mead (1934, cited in Best *et al*, 2000: 232) viewed self as a social construction arising out of social experience. While we are unique individuals this uniqueness can nevertheless only be defined and affirmed in relationships with others and the broader society. We require others to affirm or validate our own existence and we define ourselves in terms of social relationships. Telling our story is an important part of the process of defining ourselves. It is essential for our mental well-being that someone makes the time to listen and values what we have to say. Reminiscence and oral history provide a forum for this.

The role of collective memory

One of the reasons mankind has flourished as a species is our ability to communicate with each other, work co-operatively and live in social groups. Psychologists believe that one of the reasons the human brain has grown so large in comparison to those of other species is because of our need to use language and communicate with each other in order to live and work together in communities. This basic sociability and cooperativeness of mankind, with all our advances in learning, communication and technology, depends to a huge extent on the sharing of memories. Written language could never have advanced if it had not been remembered and passed from one generation to another, developing through those generations and leading to a method of sharing memories and knowledge through manuscripts, books and more recently, computers. Likewise, the laws by which we live in our societies have developed through the benefit of experience, recorded and passed on through numerous generations in the statute books. The rules by which we live as individuals and in family units contribute to the cohesiveness of society. Without them, society would disintegrate into anarchy. Advances in medicine depend on the sharing of knowledge and experience, the detailed taking of case histories and the dissemination of this knowledge through medical journals. Indeed the whole fabric of our society depends on the passing on of knowledge as each generation makes advances on that of the last, rather than having to go right back to inventing the wheel again. And what is this knowledge that is past on in verbal, written and digital form, if it is not memories? Our ability to learn from experience and to communicate that experience to others depends on our ability to remember what we have learned.

Collective memory is also essential in the development and passing on of cultural traditions. Many people think of 'culture' as something which other ethnic and religious groups have, failing to recognise that their whole view of life and morality is based on the socialisa-tion experience they have had within their own culture. This has been passed down to them subconsciously through their upbringing and social environment, and it is only with the increased mixing between, and subsequent growth in knowledge about, different cultures in modern society that our awareness of the huge influence of socialisation on each of us is growing. Older people have an essential role in passing on these traditions, and hence in maintaining the stability of society. Learning about their own cultural traditions enables younger generations to understand and respect their ethnic and religious roots, which can affirm their sense of identity and increase feelings of self-worth. For younger generations, knowing where they have come from can help to establish where they are now and assist in decision-making about which directions to take in the future. Culture gives us each a firm basis on which to stand, and a light in which to see ourselves. It can also play a part in deter-mining what we remember, as our sense of what is important in life, and therefore what needs to be registered and retained, is influenced by cultural factors. Intergenerational reminiscence is one way that family and cultural traditions can be passed on to future generations.

Intergenerational reminiscence

Intergenerational reminiscence is reminiscence work involving at least two generations of people – usually school children and older people – who come together to join in the sharing of memories and creative activities in order to learn from each other and foster positive relationships. Children's natural inquisitiveness and the enthusiasm with which they ask questions and listen to the older people has a morale-boosting effect on the latter as they realise that their life experiences are of interest to today's young people. The older learners also have the opportunity to pass on skills and knowledge which satisfies the curiosity of the children in a lively and exciting way. For instance, it may be that the closest the children have ever come to Second World War memorabilia in the past is to see them behind glass in a museum. Through intergenerational reminiscence the children not only have the opportunity to touch, handle, smell and try on such things as gas masks, but can also hear from someone who experienced what it was like to do lessons wearing gas masks whilst sitting in the school air raid shelter as part of 'gas mask drill'. This teaches today's younger generations far more about the realities of life for children in 1940s Britain than can be achieved by any amount of looking at books or watching television programmes. At the same time they learn respect for those sharing their memories and the older people themselves are likely to experience a boost of confidence through the experience of being appreciated by the young. In these circumstances, understanding between the generations grows naturally.

A rich and irreplaceable resource

Memories are a vital resource in any learning situation, as we look at new information and events in the light of our prior knowledge and experience. The whole education system in the western world depends on building on information learned previously, year after year. School children revisit particular mathematical problems time and again, each time with increasing complexity. Their understanding of quadratic equations at age fifteen depends on the simple arithmetic they first learned ten years earlier in primary school. They cannot leap straight from one to the other, but gradually build up their knowledge. Likewise, in our understanding of any new situation in life, we draw on our past experience, and once we have fully grasped this new information, we will be ready to learn still more.

One of the strengths of adult education is said to be the fact that learners are encouraged to bring the knowledge they have gained through life experiences into the classroom. This knowledge enables learners to tackle new situations with the confidence that they have mastered new skills in the past and therefore can do so again. More importantly, learners can reap the benefits of each other's experience. This is particularly so in reminiscence groups, where one learner's memories may act as a trigger to those of the rest of the group. Learners draw on one another's memories and so become a resource to each other.

Case study

A reminiscence group held in a sheltered housing complex was discussing life before the National Health Service, and how difficult it had been to afford the doctor. For a while it seemed that the group as a whole were coming to the conclusion that life had been entirely negative at that time as far as their health was concerned and that they and their families had been helpless victims of a society which did not look after its poor. During a lag in the discussion, one lady spoke up and said that they had always been very resourceful in using tradition-al remedies to good effect. This was a spark which started off a much livelier and more posi-tive discussion about the numerous ways in which people had helped themselves. Person after person recalled different remedies, some of which sounded very peculiar to the reminiscence tutor, but most of which were remembered by the whole group once their memories began to flow. Each person became a resource to the others in prompting their memories and enabling them to see how resourceful they had been in the face of illness and poverty. The mood of the group changed considerably, and several people came back the next week with written recipes for cold and flu remedies which were typed up and made into a collection for the group to keep.

Case study

Georgina Jarvis is a reminiscence tutor working for Norfolk Adult Education's 'Older People's Project' who runs a regular group for older people living in the community. On one occasion she needed to find out more about the ways in which people had practiced the 'make do and mend' philosophy of the 1940s and 50s when there was clothes rationing in Great Britain. She decided to consult the members of the reminiscence group about the things they had done, asking whether they had any information or examples of clothing which had been adjusted and reused at the time. The group talked about their memories in a limited way during the session, but then decided that they would all go away to try and find out more. During the week they asked friends and relatives, and consulted old books and magazines, coming back the next week with a wealth of examples which were not only helpful to Georgina but which sparked off a great deal of sharing of memories about blankets which had been turned into ponchos, adults' coats into children's coats, dresses into skirts, dress linings into petticoats, worn up sheets into babies' nappies and parachute silk into complete sets of underwear.

It is clear from these examples that the memories of older people are a rich resource for learning. In fact, they are a resource upon which the whole process of reminiscence depends. A reminiscence tutor with a store of knowledge about the past is not a great deal of use unless she is able to promote the sharing of memories amongst her learners. Reminiscence is a social experience as well as a learning one, and it depends on participants talking with each other about their memories. One of the great strengths of reminiscence as a learning method is that it aims to draw out this resource of memories from every member of the group. It is the memories which are the learning material, and these are provided by the learners themselves. The role of the tutor is simply to provide the triggers and the right environment in which sharing can take place. It is because of this wealth of memories, in many cases going back to the early part of the last century, that older people cannot and should not be ignored as a learning resource for people of all ages. Their memories are a storehouse of highly valuable experiences, knowledge and wisdom.

Reflection and application

1. Write a list of all the things you have done in the last twenty-four hours which have required the use of memory. What might it be like to lose this ability to remember?
2. Alone, or with others, write a list of the significant events of the twentieth century which people in your community lived through. Include local, national and international events. How might older people in your area be brought together to talk about these events? What might be the value to them, and a wider audience of recording their memories?
3. What degree of understanding and communication is there between the younger and older people living in your area? How might the younger members of your community benefit from talking to the older members about their experiences? How might the older people benefit?
4. How could you facilitate communication between older and younger members of your community through reminiscence? What might be suitable topics to base the reminiscence around?

Chapter 5

Reminiscence in adult education

Reminiscence in adult education

Reminiscence is a subject which can be undertaken by people of all ages and all abilities, although the approach taken and activities used will need to be adapted to suit the needs of particular individuals and groups. It is first and foremost about communication – of thoughts, feelings and memories – and as such is a way of expressing who we are. For many people later life brings increasing disability, which may make communication more difficult. For example, hearing impairments can make people feel socially excluded so that they may in time stop trying to understand what is being said around them. Those who have experienced strokes can find that they are no longer able to express themselves in words or writing as they once did. Sometimes, thoughts and understanding are intact in such people, but because of damage to the centres of the brain that control speech, they are not able to translate their thoughts into spoken words. Again, this can make life very lonely, especially as those around them may not realise that they have normal intelligence.

There are a number of different ways of working with people who have such impairments, such as using mime or artwork to express memories. Some items of memorabilia particularly lend themselves to mime, such as demonstrating the use of a scrubbing board or how to light a fire in a grate. Artwork can be used as a way of enabling people to indicate clothes they have worn for special occasions, or the uniform they wore during the war, as well as recreating scenes from memory such as a day out at the seaside or working life. With activities like this it is important that the reminiscence tutor introduces them sensitively, avoiding the danger of making activities like miming and drawing seem childish. By keeping the themes on adult topics, and explaining the reason for using these media to the learners, it is generally possible to enhance feelings of self-esteem and confidence by enabling communication and breaking the pattern of social isolation. The very act of showing that you believe the learners have the ability to communicate by means other than speech will encourage them to have a go at trying some alternatives.

At the other end of the scale, reminiscence can be intellectually stimulating for the more able, and can provide a challenge in rediscovering or developing skills in writing, art, handicrafts, performing arts and ICT. As shown in Chapter 2, older people generally want to have their minds stretched and their intellects challenged, and there are many ways in which reminiscence can be used in conjunction with social, political, economic and local history to expand learners' knowledge about the times and historic occasions they have lived through. In one reminiscence session, a discussion about ways of coping with food rationing during the 1940s and 1950s developed into a debate about Winston Churchill's character and political approach. The reminiscence tutor was surprised to hear some of the views expressed as they ran contrary to her understanding of Churchill's popularity during the war. As a result, many of the group members came along the next week with books and photographs showing different sides of Churchill's life and leadership. The result was an in-depth discussion in which some of the group members (and the reminiscence tutor) revised their lifelong views on Winston Churchill and the nature of the Second World War. This is also a useful example of how we all continue to learn throughout our lives, and that sometimes this can involve a process in which ideas which were once accepted as fact are cast into doubt by the benefit of hindsight and the reflections of historians and political commentators.

Using reminiscence with people with dementia

Most people, as they get older, experience what is known as benign senescent forgetfulness as a result of the gradual death of brain cells from the early twenties onwards. By the time we reach old age we are likely to be noticing the effects of this and may find that we don't take in new information or learn new skills as easily as we once did. This experience is quite different from that of a person experiencing one of the dementias, of which Alzheimer's disease is the most common. However, dementia is not as common as some people believe, with approximately one in twenty people over the age of 65 and one in five people over the age of 80 experiencing it to some degree (Alzheimer's Society, 2003). It is not an inevitable condition of later life and most people who experience it are able to live independently, or at home with assistance, until the later stages.

One of the principle symptoms of dementia is loss of memory. It tends to be short-term memory that is affected first, with memories from the late teens and early twenties being the most strongly laid down, and the last to be affected by the disease process. Many people with dementia are therefore able to talk about and enjoy memories from their earlier lives long after they have ceased to be able to communicate meaningfully about the present. Just imagine for a moment what it must be like to be in the later stages of losing your memory. You are likely to wake up each morning wondering where you are as you have come into residential care because of your memory loss. As you lie there in bed, wondering what is going on, a stranger knocks on the door and comes into the room, saying that she has come to help you get dressed. You know that you have never seen her before and resent this intrusion into your bedroom. After getting dressed you are taken to a dining area where you are given a fried breakfast. You ask for your usual porridge and are told that you always have the fried breakfast. You know that you have had porridge for breakfast all your life, but eat what has been put in front of you rather than cause a fuss. As the day progresses you are spoken to by a number of strange people you have never met before who are all extremely rude and call you by your first name, sometimes doing things to you or adjusting your clothing without asking or even speaking to you. You need the toilet, but as you are in a strange place you have no idea where it is. You ask someone, but their instructions are unintelligible. You say you want to go home and are told that this is your home. You begin to feel incompetent and extremely confused by the whole situation.

Now into this situation, bring a reminiscence tutor, bearing memorabilia relating to household tasks of the past. You immediately recognise a rag rug she is carrying as being similar to one you made with your grandmother not so very long ago, and tell her this. She asks you to explain how the rug was made and when you tell her the materials needed she pulls these out of a bag. You feel at home cutting pieces of material to size ready to peg into the Hessian. You talk as you work, telling her about your grandmother. She is obviously interested and listening, as are other people in the group. For the first time that day you feel in control of your own life. You feel capable and that you have something valid and interesting to say. Your mood and the confusion begin to lift and you feel like a whole person again. All this is because you are doing something you are familiar with and which is firmly fixed in your memory. Other people talk and listen to you and you no longer feel that you are alone in a strange world which makes no sense. When the session ends and the materials are packed away, you continue to have a feeling of well-being, although after an hour you can't remember why. You spend the rest of the day chatting to the strangers who sit near you and who move in and out of the room.

While this is a somewhat simplistic and idealist picture of how reminiscence might enhance the well-being of a person with dementia, it serves to illustrate the point that reminiscence is a useful communication technique for people with this condition who may feel alienated from their environment and unable to relate to the people around them. It cannot be said that taking part in reminiscence in any way arrests the disease process taking place in their brain, or restores cognitive functioning, but what it does do is restore their personhood. Self-confidence is built up and the ability to take part in social situations is enhanced.

Kitwood (1997) describes dementia as being made up of a number of different elements; social, psychological and biological features including:

- individual personality, including communication and social skills, and outlook on life;
- physical health and fitness;
- life experience and social history, including level of education;
- the attitudes and behaviour of people relating to the person with dementia;
- changes in the brain due to the actual dementing illness.

It is, therefore, unhelpful to put all symptoms of dementia down to the death of brain cells. Some are due to the individual's personality and how they have learned to cope with difficulties and illness throughout their life. Life history is also a significant factor as it may determine a person's ability to cope with change, as well as their outlook on life. Physical health is sometimes overlooked as a cause of psychological distress particularly where someone has difficulty in communicating. Of particular importance are the people around the person with dementia and how they relate to him. This will have a strong influence on how he sees himself. In this respect, one of the great things about reminiscence is that the reminiscence tutor approaches the person as an individual who she wants to learn about and who she believes will be able to communicate something about his past by one means or another. Reminiscence is therefore an approach which recognises and makes use of the strengths of each learner, rather than focusing on disabilities and deficits. It is a particularly relevant activity to carry out with people in the later stages of dementia because the focus is on the past, which is their area of greatest strength in terms of memory and skills. In coming into a reminiscence group people with dementia move from a world in which they are constantly asked to do things at which they fail, into one where they can succeed and where they receive acknowledgement and reinforcement for participation at any level. Reminiscence can therefore increase the well-being and raise the self-esteem and confidence of learners, whatever their cognitive abilities. The practicalities of including people with dementia in reminiscence groups are explored in Chapter 10.

Learning theories and their application to reminiscence tutoring

We shall now look at four sets of learning theories as a way of considering the contribution psychological theories can make to our understanding of how best to help older people learn through reminiscence. In each case a brief summary of the theory is given, followed by ideas on how this can be applied to reminiscence tutoring.

Behaviourist theories

On the grounds that it is not possible to observe such things as consciousness, sensation, perception and will, behaviourists confined their observation of animals and humans to objective observations of the results of stimulus and response. Decision-making and thought processes were effectively ignored, and instead, learning was defined in terms of the response to a stimulus. The experiments of behaviourists on animals in the early twentieth century led them to believe that they could build any system of behaviour in human beings by conditioning them. They thought that any pattern of behaviour could be reduced to reflexes, and learning was defined as a relatively permanent change in behaviour which could be observed and measured. B. F. Skinner argued that the learning process could be accelerated by reinforcement, defined as a stimulus which increases the probability of a response. In operant conditioning the important stimulus is that which immediately follows the response, not that which triggers it. Our behaviour is shaped by our past experience of what will happen if we behave in a particular way – whether it is rewarded or punished. However, conditioning theories fail to take into account aspects of human behaviour such as motivation and attitudinal change. Also, it is not clear how conditioning can promote the cognitive and intellectual skills which are part of intelligent thinking.

During reminiscence sessions, learners are given constant and immediate feedback by the tutor for any contribution they make in response to the memorabilia and sensory stimuli used to trigger memories. Rewards are given in the form of attention, praise and encouragement. This tends to lead to repetition of the behaviour, i.e. continued and increased participation in the session. Verbal feedback and attention can be particularly effective with learners living in residential homes, as many of them have little interaction with others on a daily basis, partly because the pressures on care staff are too great for them to stop and chat for extended periods of time.

However, learners are human beings, not robots, and they clearly make choices about when and how much to participate based on their own feelings, attitudes and motivation. For instance, some learners will choose to sit and listen rather than to talk, sometimes because they are tired, and at other times because they wish to keep their memories on a particular topic private. Rewards are not so powerful that people can be made to participate against their will.

Cognitive theories

Jean Piaget (1896–1980) believed that all children are born with innate mental structures that determine the shape of their cognitive development. These structures provide their motivation to interact with the environment and guide the growth of their knowledge about the world. He also thought the shape of the mind was affected by the environment. In contrast to the behaviourists, Piaget paid little attention to behaviour itself, but was more interested in the mental functioning that controlled behaviour. He saw mental development as passing through four clearly defined stages which led to the building up of 'mental representations' of the external world. In the course of development the child would move from being able to manipulate physical objects to manipulating objects in the mind i.e. talking and thinking about objects without having to handle them directly. The acquisition of language and the use of symbols were vital for this. Piaget is known as a 'constructivist' because he saw children as constructing their own knowledge by interacting with the environment. A related theory is 'social constructivism', developed by Lev Vygotsky (1896–1934). He saw the culture and social relationships of the child as being more important to learning than the physical environment, with those with more advanced knowledge playing an essential part in helping the child to move on to the next stage of development.

Many of the learners taking part in reminiscence suffer from cognitive impairment due to dementia. Part of their deterioration may involve loss of the ability to use language, together with an unconventional use of symbols. Understanding cognitive theories of development can

53

be useful in finding an approach to overcome the problems which arise as a result of this. Thus, while it may no longer be possible to talk to people with dementia in an abstract way about their memories, they will often respond more readily when given physical objects to hold and manipulate, for instance memorabilia relevant to their past lives. The tutor needs to adapt teaching methods to those appropriate for a more concrete level of thinking.

Vygotsky saw the people around us as having a vital role in our learning. This can frequently be seen in reminiscence tutoring on occasions when group members support and encourage each other's participation by listening, asking questions and adding their own comments. It is the social relationships that are vital to the learning process in a group functioning in this way, rather than a directive role played by the tutor.

Gestalt theories

Gestalt learning takes place when we restructure a problem in our mind to see how the whole thing might work. Kohler (1887–1967) called it 'insight learning'. It involves visualising a problem in a new way, and seeing how the different bits make sense together. Seeing the whole process helps to make sense of the parts. Gestaltists see learning as a dynamic process – a creative restructuring which arises from thinking problems through. The capacity for creative thinking will be present in most learners. This capacity is in the learner and is to be brought out. It is not in the tutor to be conveyed to the learner by some technique of knowledge transfer. A key factor in insight learning is that the learners are encouraged to discover the answers for themselves, rather than being told them.

The factors which distinguish insight learning are:

- the solution is a sudden leap, as if pieces were fitting together;
- once it has been accomplished, it is easier to solve similar problems;
- it leads to permanence in learning, and we can transfer that learning to unfamiliar situations in different contexts.

Part of the process of adapting to the change and loss often brought about through ageing is looking back on how life has been as a whole. Reminiscence can play an important part in assisting people to make sense of their lives. Looking back over the entire lifespan can help to make sense of how it all fits together, and what the meanings of present experiences are. This can lead to a greater sense of well-being and self-acceptance, and an ability to cope with the uncertainty of the future.

The reminiscence process involves experiential learning through sensory stimulation and handling objects of memorabilia. These evoke memories which can be relived in the mind, in such a way that new conclusions can be reached about life's experiences. Learners have to reach this new insight about the value of their lives themselves – they cannot learn it by being told it by a tutor. Likewise, a reminiscence tutor does not handle objects and tell learners what they are like, but passes them round for people to experience for themselves.

Humanist theories

Abraham Maslow described a hierarchy of human needs that are necessary for growth. For the higher level needs to be reached, the lower level needs must first be satisfied. At the lowest level are physiological needs. These are followed by safety needs, belongingness and love needs, esteem needs, and at the top, self-actualisation, which is the realisation of an individual's full potential. A person's position within the hierarchy can change all the time. In order to be able to teach people, their physiological and safety needs must first be met, otherwise concerns about these will dominate their thinking.

Many of the learners in reminiscence groups live in residential care where physiological and safety needs are mostly met by care staff, but where higher-order needs can sometimes be neglected. Reminiscence groups provide an environment in which learners can feel that they belong and have value. Self-esteem grows as they find that their memories are treated with respect and are considered important by the tutor and other group members.

It is a sad fact that many people have a very limited view of the potential of older people, particularly once they are living in residential care. In reality, there is no reason why older people, frail and with disabilities, nearing the end of their lives, should not find the same fulfilment, truth and understanding as younger people. The right conditions for older people to grow and flourish are described by Carl Rogers in his person-centred approach. He believed that human beings have a natural propensity to learning, especially when they feel safe and see the relevance of the material. The person-centred approach advocates seeing each person as an individual with a unique combination of needs and abilities. For learning to be most effective it has to be right for that individual at that time.

In reminiscence the individuality and uniqueness of the memories of each learner are valued and nurtured. Nobody is forced to participate if they don't want to, and all activities are adapted to be as relevant as possible to the life experiences of the learners. The fact that learning usually takes place in small groups makes this adaptation to the needs of individuals easier. The tutor responds in a respectful, genuine and empathetic way, showing each learner the unconditional positive regard considered so vital for growth by Rogers.

Learning styles and reminiscence activities
Each learner is different and has preferred ways of working and communicating. The range of activities which can be incorporated into a reminiscence class is vast and it is likely that there will be something that appeals to most learners within any one session. Chapter 6 deals with a range of different creative activities, while this chapter looks at the use of the five senses and movement, making it suitable for people who like to learn using visual, auditory, tactile and kinaesthetic styles.

Visual learning
This style suggests that the learner has a preference for information presented visually and through pictures. Slides, videos, photographs, old newspapers, post cards, maps and plans are all good triggers to use. These learners may be particularly good at visualising scenes from the past in their minds which can then be expressed through art.

Auditory learning
Learners who prefer this style tend to like to learn through speaking and listening, and so will benefit from taking part in group discussions or listening to taped sounds, such as steam trains, famous historic speeches or music. When trying to remember something, they can often hear the way it was said to them, and can therefore be good mimics of others. They tend to repeat whole conversations with significant people from decades ago, which can be fascinating and entertaining to the whole group. Reading poetry and singing songs from the past can bring back many memories.

Tactile/kinaesthetic learning

Learners who prefer this style tend to be most actively engaged when they can touch, feel and use objects and when they are physically active within the learning environment. Memorabilia of all sorts are most attractive to these learners, particularly where they have moving parts, or can be mimed with to demonstrate their use. Textiles (such as leather, fur and velvet) are useful with tactile learners as the different textures evoke memories when handled. Procedural memories such as making pastry and peeling potatoes can be familiar activities from the past which are no longer available to learners living in residential or nursing homes, and would therefore be appreciated. Such activities can be introduced as part of talking about cooking in the past.

Ratey (2001) describes how physical movements can assist the ability to think, learn and remember:

> It has been shown that certain physical activities which have a strong mental component... enhance social, behavioural, and academic abilities. Although the reasons are not completely understood, many reports indicate that this is so. Evidence is mounting that each person's capacity to master new and remember old information is improved by biological changes in the brain brought on by physical activity. (Ratey, 2001: 278)

This suggests that using movement during reminiscence sessions will facilitate the reminiscence process, leading to more social interaction in the group, fewer behaviour problems, and a greater willingness and ability to learn from each other.

Smell and taste

As well as sight, hearing, touch and movement, the senses of smell and taste can also evoke strong memories for some learners, thus aiding their participation in reminiscence. The smell and taste of freshly baked bread is evocative for most people, but the aroma of flowers, freshly mown grass, coal and sawn wood may also bring back memories, as may the taste of fruits, sweets and peas fresh from the pod, familiar from childhood. These memories can sometimes be combined with tactile and kinaesthetic memories through having a baking session, or where facilities for this do not exist making some non-cook sweets. It is not always necessary to have the actual smell or taste to hand in order to trigger memories, as the Karen case study shows.

Case study

Karen was a reminiscence tutor working with a group of six residents in a nursing home. During the first session she seemed to be getting nowhere with them. She had tried starting a discussion by passing round memorabilia and photographs and playing music from the 1940s. Nobody was responding to anything with more than one- or two-word answers. Collecting her thoughts she decided to try the sense of smell as a trigger. Having nothing with her in the way of aromas, she drew the group's attention to her and said: 'Imagine you are a child. You can be whatever age you like up to about 15. You have just come in from school and opened the front door. What can you smell? You walk through to the kitchen where someone is cooking. What does the food smell like? Take a deep breath and draw in the aroma of your childhood home. Just sit with that smell, breathing it in for a few minutes'. Once a few minutes had past, Karen asked the group to share what they had smelt, and one by one every member of the group shared their memories, starting with the smells and going on to describe what and who they had seen in their homes. The imagined smells were the trigger for other memories to come flooding out. The rest of the session, and course, were much livelier having made this initial breakthrough.

Right and left brain dominance and the sharing of memories

In the 1950s and 1960s Roger Sperry carried out research into the different activities of the left and right sides of the brain. It was found that the brain divided different tasks between the hemispheres and that when one hemisphere is active the other is in a relatively restful state. Left-brain activities were generally labelled as more academic, intellectual and business-like, whilst right-brain activities were those which are more artistic, creative and emotional. In looking at the relative strengths in learning of people with right or left brain dominance, it was considered that the following skills were apparent:

Left hemisphere dominant	**Right hemisphere dominant**
Has a good short-term memory	Relies on highly personal associations to remember.
Thinks in words	Thinks in images
Remembers sequences	Remembers patterns
Takes in information step by step in a logical sequence.	Takes in parts in terms of whole
Looks for cause and effect	Looks for simultaneous connections
Relies on induction and analysis	Is adept at synthesis and intuitive links
Is time conscious	Is space conscious

Research since the 1970s has shown that people can be trained to use their non-dominant hemisphere and that by doing so they can increase the overall functioning of their brain. This is thought to be what the great creative geniuses of history have done (Buzan, 2001). Using both intellect and imagination they have been able to look beyond the limitations of the available knowledge of their time and come up with new inventions and scientific theories which

57

have eventually brought us to where we are today. Whilst acknowledging that learners are likely to be either left- or right-brain dominant, and will therefore find some methods of learning easier than others, it is important to try and develop the skills associated with both hemispheres of the brain. Thus, in reminiscence, tutors can appeal to left-hemisphere strengths through using words in discussion, on tape and in reading; they can use a linear way of thinking in talking about dates and looking at the events of the past in the order in which they happened; and they can create lists of local cinemas, makes of perfume, and styles of dress which have existed in the past. At the same time they can appeal to right-hemisphere strengths by using lots of shapes, colours and textures in the memorabilia, using music and art, creativity and imagination, and by encouraging people to look back on their lives as a whole.

At a time of life when cognitive skills may be weakening, it is essential to the well-being of older people to use as much of their brains as possible. Reminiscing is an ideal way of stimulating the mind in that it uses such a wide range of activities which draw on both the left and right hemispheres of the brain.

Using reminiscence to enhance literacy skills

Learners studying with Norfolk Adult Education's 'Additional Learning Support' team, which works largely with people with learning disabilities, use reminiscence in courses on local history and the 1960s. While these courses generally reach younger adults, learners are able to undertake their own research by asking parents, neighbours and friends what life was like in their town or village in previous decades. In one local history group for people with mild to moderate learning disabilities, learners used drawings and written text to describe the villages and towns where they lived. This gave them opportunities for learning more about their own communities as well as choosing some of their favourite places to visit, draw and write about. Music, entertainment, fashions, transport and home life of the past are all considered on these courses, with learners adding their memories about their own childhoods. Colourful drawings, photos and written text are then used to record what they have learned. On one course, learners look at, handle and describe memorabilia which was in common use in previous decades. Items are classified in terms of the materials they are made from and their use, thus increasing learners' knowledge of changes in manufacturing and industry over the past century, as well as their understanding of how everyday life has changed.

One group of learners in Cromer, whose intellectual achievements and abilities were particularly low, was visited by a reminiscence tutor who talked with them about the Second World War as part of their local history class. It was possible to fit this in with the learning already undertaken by the class by showing how and where it fitted into Cromer's history. It also gave group members the opportunity to contribute their own knowledge by telling each other stories of wartime experiences which they had heard from parents and grandparents. These stories were then used as part of the literacy work the class did as they wrote down a summary of what they had learned. Amongst the memorabilia which the reminiscence tutor took along were a number of items of military clothing. The learners enjoyed trying these on, especially the caps and helmets, and were able to gain some understanding of what it felt like to be a soldier in uniform. This experience inspired their writing and gave them greater enthusiasm for the subject. Though none of this group of learners was old enough to have lived through the war, sharing memories and listening to the memories of others gave them a glimpse into the reality of what life had been like at that time. In subsequent sessions the class was taken to see places where there had been bombing in Cromer, and read accounts of other people's memories.

Reminiscence and Skills for Life

Heather Myhill is a tutor with Norfolk Adult Education Service who is qualified to teach both reminiscence and Skills for Life. Heather uses learners' memories to enhance basic literacy skills in two ways:

1) Themed reminiscence courses

The aim of these courses is to improve basic literacy skills, but this is linked to reminiscence. People who are not aware that they have basic skills needs, or who are unwilling to turn up and admit that they have difficulty with reading, writing or spelling, are no longer pushed into the position of having to present themselves from the beginning as having difficulties in these areas. There can be many reasons for having missed out on acquiring these skills when young, such as not attending school, either through truanting or having no choice (many people in their sixties and seventies had their schooling interrupted by the war) or through not being ready to learn when young. It is a major thing for people who have got to later life to admit that they have literacy problems. On these themed courses, while other skills are being taught literacy skills are addressed at the same time. At the end of the course learners take the National Literacy Test. The fact that the aim of the course is to teach literacy skills is explained from the start, when learners attend a two hour taster course. However, reminiscence is used as the vehicle through which to teach the literacy skills and this helps to build up learners' confidence, drawing attention away from any shame they may feel about their difficulties with literacy.

Case study

Heather Myhill worked with a group of learners on a themed reminiscence course in Swaffham, Norfolk. This group produced a book of their war memories which is now in the local library. A copy of the book is also used by a local school to teach children about the Second World War as part of their GCSE History and English curricula. This brings the war to life for the young people, showing them its reality in the lives of local people.

All members of the themed reminiscence group have now taken their National Literacy Tests at both Levels 1 and 2, and the class is continuing as a creative writing group. Learners are now producing a collection of short stories which they hope to get published. The degree to which the confidence of the learners has grown is indicated in the fact that the group also gives talks to children about their experiences.

2) Embedded skills courses

Hanni John, Skills for Life Manager with Norfolk Adult Education Service, explains that in true embedding there would be two tutors working alongside each other – one with a qualification in reminiscence and one with a Skills for Life teaching qualification. Each course would have two sets of learning outcomes and at the end two certificates would be awarded if these planned outcomes have been fulfilled – one for literacy skills and one for reminiscence skills. At the moment embedded courses in Norfolk use just one tutor and work within a subject context which is of interest to learners.

In planning embedded courses, Heather Myhill gives equal weighting to reminiscence and basic skills learning, so that learners can attend one class where the two skills are taught together. The classes start with learners sharing their memories because they are interested in the past. They are then taught the skills necessary for writing the memories down, such as spelling, sentence structure and grammar. On these courses learners do not take the National Literacy Test at the end, as the main aim is to enable them to record their memories literately. They are taught the appropriate words and methods for doing what they want to do, which are related to recording their memories and family history. These skills are transferable, in that having improved their spelling, sentence structure and grammar, they can then use them in everyday life.

It is hoped that true embedding of Skills for Life will be used on reminiscence courses in Norfolk in the near future. Such a course might be 40 hours long, consisting of 20 hours of reminiscence and 20 hours of literacy skills. However, the literacy skills would be taught in the context of reminiscence and would still be related to the reminiscence skills. This is a highly motivating way to learn as the learners are already interested in the subject, the learning is more enjoyable than in traditional literacy classes and learning takes place at a faster pace because the new skills are applied immediately. These skills can then be transferred to other situations such as writing to grandchildren, reading books or using e-mail. Older people also find that with enhanced literacy skills they are better able to get involved in their communities through volunteering and campaigning, as well as through passing on accurate facts to their grandchildren.

Reflection and application

1. What sensory stimuli for sight, sound, touch, taste and smell might trigger memories of your own childhood?
2. Where might you acquire the knowledge and resources for sensory triggers for people whose country of origin is different to your own?
3. What differences might there be in appropriate memory triggers for people from different parts of your own region or town? Do you have minority cultural, ethnic or religious groups living nearby who may be excluded from full participation in reminiscence groups by the use of triggers which appeal to the majority of older people in your area?
4. Reflect on ways in which reminiscence could be used to enhance an adult literacy programme running in your area. How might the inclusion of reminiscence activities open up adult literacy classes to a wider audience?
5. What might be the 'rewards' of reminiscence for group facilitators and participants? How might this effect motivation to learn?

Chapter 6

Creativity and memories

Creativity and memories

Memories are inherently creative in that when a person remembers something they call up a sensory image in their mind of what they have experienced and re-create that experience within themselves. Memories are laid down in all sensory modalities – sight, hearing, touch, taste and smell, as well as movement – and when a memory is recalled, it is as though the experience is lived over again within the individual's mind. This requires imagination, and the more imaginative a person is, the more likely it is that their perception of the past will be sufficiently enhanced to be able to produce images which other people can appreciate in art, drama, music, dance, creative writing or crafts.

For some people who have had traumatic experiences this can cause problems, as they may continue to see and hear the images which originally traumatised them. Such occurrences need to be dealt with by the reminiscence tutor, and should never be ignored or brushed under the carpet. However, it is rarely appropriate to put a person's traumatic memories on public display, and so this chapter deals almost exclusively with more positive memories.

Although talking about the past can in itself be a beneficial activity, there are further benefits to be gained from taking reminiscence into a more creative stage. The level of sharing deepens as group members produce visual and auditory images of their experiences. The memories themselves move from being within the individual's mind to being 'on the page' – something which can be shared, passed around and commented on. As such, it can feel like a great risk to put memories into a more tangible form, and learners often need additional encouragement to begin this creative process. Apart from this possible perceived threat to privacy involved in revealing memories in an external form, some older learners may suffer from the effects of having been told at school that they 'could not draw/act/sing'. This is likely to have deeply affected their confidence about their abilities throughout their lives, and can be compounded in the face of physical or sensory impairments which have accrued through the ageing process. However, with the assistance and encouragement of a positively focused tutor, who sees what the learners can, rather than what they cannot do, most people can eventually find some form of creative expression which enhances their ability to communicate their life experiences and identity.

Some of the benefits of creativity in later life are:

- **Creativity affirms identity.** Once the initial embarrassment of acting or drawing is overcome, most people find creative expression an effective way of being able to communicate who they are and what they feel about their life experiences, as well as their aspirations and hopes for the future.

- **Creativity is pleasurable.** Human beings are inherently creative, and there is something about the creative process which often makes people feel more fully human. This inherent creativity is often taken away from people when they are young by misguided teachers and parents who dampen their creativity by surrounding it with prohibitions – 'don't splash paint on the table', 'don't talk to your friends while you are writing your story', 'that's not poetry it doesn't rhyme'. The learner-centred and non-judgemental attitude of the reminiscence tutor can provide freedom for older people to re-discover their natural talent for creativity – and enjoy doing so! This can have a profound effect on well-being in later life as learners discover the significance of their unique contributions, and as a result experience increasingly positive feelings about themselves and the lives they have lived, and are living.

- **Creativity enhances and develops skills.** Writing, painting, dancing and acting are all activities involving skills which can be developed through practice. This can lead to increased confidence in the individual, as well as greater pleasure in the activity – for both performer and audience. Having a finished product or performance is something which learners can focus on, take pride in, and show off about – all essential elements in moving away from seeing older people as passive recipients of care. The creative process enables learners to work on a product which they can give to others, as well as being something which they take part in for their own pleasure.

- **Creativity leads to deeper sharing and co-operation.** When a group of older learners works together to turn memories into a product, be it a performance or a book of memories, they have a stronger sense of purpose in sharing their memories which can lead to a deeper level of communication and involvement with each other. Co-operation and interaction between group members is thus enhanced and is likely to lead to the deepening of friendships and understanding between people. The process of planning the creative product is also likely to enrich skills in imaginative thinking and the communication of ideas. As learners share their ideas and memories, these are likely to spark off those of other learners, so that each older person becomes a resource to the others. Faced with the question 'Do you remember...?' most people will find their minds go blank, but listening to others reminiscing can trigger memories and make it easier to express them. Using memories for a creative purpose heightens the sense of their significance, leading to an increase in self-esteem for anyone involved in the discussion and subsequent productivity.

- **The products of creativity can brighten and refresh environments.** Care homes and day centres can sometimes seem quite cold and clinical environments, far from welcoming to newcomers and visitors. This can be transformed by the display of art work and crafts produced by residents and members. This is also an important part of allowing older people to put their mark on a place, thus enhancing their sense of belonging. Seeing artwork and photos of activities on the walls of dayrooms and corridors can be effective memory prompts for those suffering from dementia as they recall the part they played in producing pictures and collages, as well as re-triggering the original memory that inspired the piece. It also contributes to turning venues into more stimulating and interesting environments, and provides material for conversation for friends and family as well as staff and residents.

- **Creative activity can bring improvements to physical and mental health.** A creative activity such as dance can not only inspire and draw on the imagination of older learners, but is also likely to have beneficial effects for their health. Dance is one of the best forms of exercise and can be undertaken by people with quite profound levels of disability. Physical activity in response to the rhythm of a piece of music exercises any part of the body which can be moved, whether this involves taking part in a waltz or just moving hands and arms in time to the music. For people who spend much of their lives stationary, even a limited amount of movement will increase the flow of oxygen to the brain and thus improve mental alertness. Dancing to music is an enjoyable activity which brings back memories of first hearing the piece as well as inspiring movement through the rhythm. Singing too, is good exercise for the lungs, and often includes people who can join in few other forms of activity. Even after losing the power of speech, some people with severe dementia can still sing their favourite hymns from beginning to end. In fact most forms of reminiscence involve some form of physical activity at a greater level than is demanded during the average day of life in a residential home. Lifting and passing objects, miming their use, and talking animatedly about memories all involve the whole person. Creative reminiscence just takes these activities one step further by encouraging a higher level of expression.

- **Creativity provides opportunities for making choices.** Many older people begin by saying that they cannot do anything creative, but once they join in, find that they love the sessions. While groups are kept fun and relaxed, a certain amount of structure enables people to make the choices which will lead to greater self expression and autonomy. Decisions can be made about what colours to use and how to apply them. There are opportunities to learn about colour mixing and every time this is done a choice is made about what shades to make. Most people, once they have had a go and found out how effective their efforts are, are keen to return for future sessions.

Creativity and intergenerational reminiscence

Claire Kerrison is a reminiscence tutor who specialises in intergenerational and creative reminiscence. She has worked as an activities co-ordinator in a nursing home for older people where residents had both physical and cognitive impairments. Whilst working at this nursing home Claire felt it would be a good idea to get local schools involved in the creative reminiscence work she was doing with residents. She approached two local schools and found the head teachers enthusiastic about involving the children.

A group of six 7- to 8-year-olds from one school came each week and were matched with six residents, drawn from the groups of older people with physical and mental impairments. Initially, time was spent using games to help the schoolchildren and residents get to know each other. They moved on to more creative activities, with each older person working in a pair with one child. All six pairs worked together in creating a collage of their names using a variety of materials and methods of applying paint. A banner was created with everyone's name on it, creating a sense of group identity.

In co-operation with teachers from the school, one of the aims of this project was to link the work done at the nursing home with material from the school curriculum. In this way the children could deepen their learning by interacting with the older people and then relay what they heard to the rest of the class. One topic covered was the Second World War. The children had started looking at this in class and benefited from the residents' first-hand accounts of rationing, the blackout and life in the Forces. With the help of a reminiscence tutor, Claire recorded the war memories of several of the residents at the home, and then a visit was made to the school where the older people read out their memories. This boosted their self-esteem as well as significantly deepening the children's understanding about the realities of the Second World War. It brought the history lesson to life, underlining the fact that these things had happened to real people who still remember them. The war-time accounts were also made into a book of memories which was left in the reception at the home so that visitors could read it.

As part of another project, the children and older people looked together at the history of toys. Both older and younger learners brought a favourite toy to the session and Claire provided examples of toys from the past such as a whip and top, hoopla and skipping rope. A 'hop scotch' pitch was drawn out on a large sheet of paper and older learners described and demonstrated the use of some of these games to the younger learners. The group as a whole talked about how toys and games had changed over time, and then worked together in pairs to make colourful peg dolls and wooden spinners. Residents benefited from taking on the role

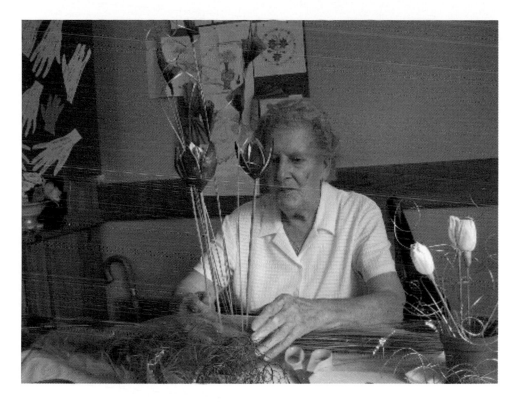

of teacher in these activities. The hands-on approach to demonstrating their knowledge was particularly well suited to some of the older people whose verbal skills were impaired.

During a painting to music session a track by Glen Miller was played, setting the mood for an enjoyable session where the pairs worked together on pictures inspired by the music. They were not directed in any way, other than to be told that they did not have to produce a picture that looked like anything – it was more about making their mark. Residents and children made decisions together about which colours to use and how to mark the paper. The resulting paintings were colourful and eye-catching. It was a good opportunity for both generations of learners to express their individuality through making choices, at the same time as working co-operatively with each other. The pictures were framed and put up on the wall. Weeks later, residents with cognitive impairments were still pointing at the pictures and telling staff and visitors about the session.

As part of the school curriculum, children and older learners looked together at local historic buildings. This was a topic on which the older people could contribute their local knowledge. Claire took photos of old buildings in Norwich, and used pictures in books which illustrated the stained glass windows and architecture of Norwich cathedral. Working in pairs, the learners chose their designs and drew them. They then made a design in clay which was made into a cast using Plaster of Paris. After being painted the designs were divided between the school and the nursing home so that everyone could benefit from what was produced.

A group of dancers from Zimbabwe came to the school to perform to the children as part of their study of African culture. Older and younger learners joined together to make African masks for the occasion. The residents attended the session at the school where storytelling was intermixed with dancing, and comparisons were drawn between the lifestyles of typical

African children and young Westerners, as well as between the lives of young people in Britain today and in the past. The older learners were able to contribute to this discussion by reminiscing about their own childhoods as well as learning more about African culture. The younger learners were able to see clear differences between their lives and both the past in their own country and the present in African countries. The children and older people joined in the dancing as far as they were able, and at the end of the day everyone was invited to dance together in a 'celebration of life'. All the participants enthused about the whole experience for weeks afterwards.

Each group of six children came for a period of six weeks so that everyone in the class had a chance to join a project. All residents were given the opportunity to join in, but nobody was made to take part against their will. As it turned out, everyone who joined the projects enjoyed working with the children and close relationships were formed with some children visiting residents long after their involvement with the project was over. The benefits of intergenerational creativity projects were seen to work both ways – for old and for young.

Work with a second school focused mostly on music and drama. Beginning with singing sessions, a small group of children were joined by an equal number of older people. It was a genuinely inclusive activity with no judgements being made about the quality of anyone's singing. Songs were chosen which were familiar to the older people and could easily be learnt by the children. Together they made up mimes to songs such as 'I'm forever blowing bubbles', 'Cockles and mussels', and 'Daisy, Daisy'. The children learnt the songs quickly and practiced them during school hours so that the combined effort made by the two groups was impressive.

A performance for the rest of the home was prepared for the summer fete. One lady of 94 sang a solo of 'I'm forever blowing bubbles' which was enjoyed by the whole audience. On reflection it was felt that every member of the group gained from the experience. Most of the older people had never performed in public before and it was a great boost to their confidence and self-esteem. The intergenerational work had enabled old and young to see themselves in a new light and to recognise that they had abilities and skills which might otherwise have remained undiscovered. This was apart from the increase in understanding which grew between the generations, the enjoyment of the activities and the knowledge which was gained through listening to each other and drawing on one another's experience.

Claire moved on to carry out further intergenerational work with fifteen year olds in Aylsham, a small market town in Norfolk. This project brought together residents of a sheltered housing complex and pupils from the local High School to look at the history of Aylsham, and produce a map showing the past and present of the town. The first time the older and younger learners met, they each jotted down the activities they used their hands for, both now and in the past. A collage was produced in which the memories of old and young were mixed together, showing the huge variety of activities in which the group had been involved. Creating the collage was a co-operative process, and in comparing activities several similarities and contrasts were found, as well as providing opportunities for sharing life experiences. This activity introduced both age groups to the idea of thinking about differences between past and present so that they could then think more creatively about how to produce a map showing the history of their town. Claire emphasised the importance of the map being the creation of the group acknowledging that the best ideas came from them working together.

One of the problems in today's society is that we are no longer so intergenerational in our social and family groups. With increasing family breakdown and movement around the country to find work, young people are less likely to see their grandparents and so feel less comfortable in the presence of older people than might have been the case in the past. Also, the image of young people created by the media has left many older people fearful of the young they encounter in public places. Through intergenerational reminiscence work, both young and old embark on a new learning journey, discovering new information, new opportunities and new talents in a fun and interesting way as they work together. Young and old share their experiences and appreciate the fact that people are listening to them and asking questions. Many older people delight in the inquisitiveness of this younger appreciative audience, and the younger people are interested in a source of information which is 'alive and real' in a way that books, videos and television aren't. Intergenerational work is especially important in keeping a sense of life and vitality in residential and nursing homes by bringing in a section of the community which is usually kept outside – the young. Many residents are not able to get outside the home and see the full spectrum of human society, but through these projects the community can come to them.

Reminiscence and Arts and Crafts

Most people will have used their hands for something creative at some time in their lives – whether this was for cooking, gardening, carpentry, knitting or sewing. This is quite apart from those who may have been talented artists and simply need encouragement to try their hand at painting or drawing again. Reminiscence tutors may be afraid of upsetting people with acquired impairments which prevent them from producing such good results as in the past. Fearing that they will be reminded about what they have lost, it may seem better for them not to take part. Rather than giving up totally on a hobby they once enjoyed these people can be encouraged to develop a new style, experimenting with new techniques and materials.

There are a number of crafts for which materials are readily available which can produce good results using simple techniques. Card making, glass painting and silk painting can be used alongside discussions about the crafts people have done in the past, as well as reminiscence about art and craft classes at school. There is always a balance to be achieved between enjoying the process of making something and having a presentable product. Some people worry much more about the product than others, and will not be satisfied unless the finished item is perfect. This can be difficult where people have disabilities such as arthritis, tremor or hemiplegia which limit the use of their hands. However, some simple steps can ensure that the finished product is not only their work but is also satisfactory to them. Firstly, *plan* what is going to be done, and think together with the older learner about what is the best way to go about it given their disabilities. If the task they want to complete will be too difficult for them to do alone then you need to negotiate which bits each of you is going to do. It might be that the only help they need is with holding something still or getting the tops off paint pots. Secondly, make sure that they are not *unnecessarily disabled*. For instance, do they usually wear glasses for close-up work, or would a thicker or shorter paint brush be easier for them to hold? Could the paint be put in a more accessible container? Have they got enough workspace and is their chair at the right height relative to the table? Thirdly, use the best possible *quality of materials*. It is sometimes the case that a finished product doesn't look as good as it could because the materials used are of low quality. Even the best artists would have some difficulty producing quality pictures with a set of children's paints! Papier-mâché done with old newspapers generally shows the newsprint even after it has been painted, and therefore detracts from what could be a good finished product. Plain paper is always best. Even with good quality paints, a picture will only look its best if done with good quality brushes on the appropriate type of paper i.e. watercolour paper for watercolours and acrylic paper for acrylics.

These are all simple tips which can help to improve the product, and so increase the overall enjoyment of taking part in creative activities. Experience also shows that when working with people with dementia it is not a good idea to offer too much choice. While some choice in materials is essential, if the range is too great the whole session will be taken up with indecision and anxiety over what to use. The best way to introduce variety is to offer a small but different range of materials each week.

In a 'Drawing on your Memories' group in Norfolk, the format is to spend half an hour at the beginning looking at and handling memorabilia on a particular theme (e.g. dressing up to go out), and talking about memories associated with this. Memorabilia might include photos of fashions from the 1930s and 1940s, items of make-up and jewellery, hats and clothes. Learners talk about their memories from that time and how they would dress up for special occasions, what these occasions might be, and the people they associate with those times. The opportunity is then given for each of the learners to produce their own piece of artwork inspired by the preceding discussion. About thirty minutes is allowed for this to be done. Finally, the group comes together for another thirty minutes and each person describes what they have drawn or painted and the memories that are captured in the picture. This last section of reminiscing can inspire ideas for future sessions as well as providing the opportunity for sharing in greater depth. As learners focus on a single memory for the thirty minutes in which they are drawing, many more memories may be triggered. The drawing process allows them to pause for a while and let their thoughts dwell on one particular aspect of their lives. The result is a much deeper level of sharing at the end of the group and subsequent enhanced understanding and communication. In using this approach it is the *creative process* rather than the finished product which is important to intensifying the reminiscence experience and increasing the sharing of memories. Some learners will still be pleased (or displeased) with their pictures, but the important thing is the reminiscing and the group interaction which has been aided by the act of creating a picture.

Some people with very little comprehensible speech can communicate more clearly when they have painted or drawn something relating to their memories. It becomes easier to describe a memory when its image is in front of them rather than inside their heads. People with dementia who are usually quite restless can become considerably calmer when they are engaged in drawing pictures related to their memories. For a short interval they are able to focus on one thing without getting lost in the maze of their thoughts. The unfolding picture brings them back time and time again to the same memory rather than wandering from one thought to the next. Generally, these sessions, although centred around one theme, inspire completely different memories in each learner, so that a wide variety of pictures and a wide range of memories have been discussed by the end of the session. Using this 'drawing on memories' format has been found to be successful in encouraging people to join in who usually find it difficult to talk in a group. However, it is equally applicable to more able learners who can use the time to explore their memories in more depth and come to a greater understanding of the significance of these memories within the context of their whole lives.

Reminiscence and creative writing

Creative writing based on the memories of older people includes recounting autobiographical stories, writing fiction set in the past and writing poetry inspired by reminiscing. Some learners have been inspired to write their own life history after participating in short interviews about their wartime experiences with members of Norfolk Adult Education's reminiscence team. Many more people have thought about doing this, and would do so, if given the right support and encouragement. As discussed in Chapter 1, there is currently a growing interest in oral history, and the publication of autobiographical accounts from people who have lived through events of historical significance is a growing industry. In the wake of the publicity surrounding the 60th anniversary of the end of the Second World War, a number of books which draw on the experiences of ordinary people have been published.

Age Exchange in Blackheath, London has published several books consisting entirely of everyday memories of life in the past. These include books on going to the seaside, medical care before the NHS, and life in the 1920s and 1930s. On the whole, these memories are not written down by the older people themselves, but are drawn from recorded interviews which are then transcribed and edited. Interviewees are involved in the whole process and given a central role in decision making about the use of vernacular language and grammar.

There are a number of reasons why it is sometimes better to use interviews and transcription, rather than expecting the older person to write down their memories themselves. These include the physical frailty and sensory impairments which affect many people in later life which may make it physically impossible for them to write their own memoirs. There is also the fact that some older people have difficulties with literacy because of lack of opportunities in education in the past, or misguided methods of teaching in the early twentieth century which eroded their confidence in their literacy skills. There is also a factor of time, as writing takes longer than speaking, and some older people may not have sufficient energy for enough hours of the day to undertake the writing of their life histories.

Members at a day centre in Norwich have recently taken part in creating a 'Book of Memories' with the help of two Age Exchange project workers. Rather than focusing on the lives of individuals, the group members looked at a number of items of memorabilia and talked about their memories of such things as a scrubbing board and a flat iron, or of helping their mothers with the baking. The completed 'Book of Memories' consists of a number of sections divided according to the items of memorabilia which inspired those memories. Rather than putting the emphasis on a particular person, this method of recording memories meant that the finished product was a group effort which recorded the variety of uses the different items had. This was also found to be an extremely effective way of fostering good relationships between group members as they had a feeling of group ownership of the final 'book'.

A group of eight older people with severe physical and cognitive impairments worked together to make up a fictional story over a number of weeks. The process began with the reminiscence tutor providing a selection of memorabilia to choose from and each learner picking out one item, saying why they had chosen it. The group then discussed how the items could be linked together in one story by looking at what sort of person might use, buy or possess each of the items. A great deal of imagination was used in constructing a character who might have some link with each item, and after two weeks of working on the story the tutor was able to present a typed version of the events described by the learners. The final session was used to provide illustrations for each page of the story with learners working on one picture each using fabrics, lace, ribbons and paints, which were then bound into a single volume with the printed pages. Again, this method of working together on a project was effective in improving communication and deepening relationships between group members.

Many older people are familiar with poetry, having had to learn it by heart at school. While they may be happy to recite poems, most people are somewhat hesitant when it comes to writing poetry. One method of introducing learners to poetry writing is to get them to write a group poem. Begin by warming up the group with reminiscing on a particular theme, for instance, memories of the seaside. Memorabilia such as shells, sand, bucket and spade, ice cream wafers and seaweed can be used to trigger memories. As poetry is a particularly sensory form of writing, it is important that the group is encouraged to think in terms of the sights, sounds, smells, tastes and tactile sensations of the seaside. Here are examples of the ideas one group came up with when talking about the sensory experiences of the seaside:

Tastes of the seaside:
fish and chips; ice cream;
crabs; shrimps;
sand sandwiches!

Things to feel at the sea:
cold water; melting ice cream;
crunchy sand to walk on;
cool breeze; donkey's fur.

Smells of the seaside:
salt air; fish; donkeys.

Sounds of the seaside:
sea gulls crying; Punch and Judy;
the swish-swish of waves;
the fun-fair.

Things to see at the sea:
caravans; boats; crabs;
fog & mist; fun-fair;
starfish; shells.

This is a useful exercise in itself as a way of getting learners to remember the time they spent on the beach as children or young adults. From here, you can move on to the poetry writing exercise. Each person is encouraged to write down, on a separate piece of paper in about fifteen words, one memory of going to the beach which particularly stands out in their mind. When everyone has done this, the group places all the pieces of paper in any order in the centre of the table and they are all read out. In order for the final poem to be fully owned by the group, their full participation in the next stage is essential. Here, learners decide together the order in which the pieces of paper will be placed to create the poem. Below is the poem written by the group which compiled the list of seaside sensory experiences. The poem does not rhyme, and doesn't meet many of the other rules of poetry. However, what it does do is 'paint a picture in words', which is as good a definition of poetry as any other.

Happy Memories of the Sea
The warm glow of the sun baking the sand
as I play on the beach with friends;
making sand-castles and
drawing pictures in the sand.
Buying ice creams from the market place
with carefully saved pocket money.
The waves washing in and out;
in and out.
Watching the sun fade over the sea:
all yellows and reds.
My family gathered together,
having fun.

Reminiscence and drama

There is a wide range of activities where drama can be used as a way of expressing learners' memories. These include miming the use of items of memorabilia – an activity which can be effective with people in the later stages of dementia who may have difficulty expressing themselves in speech. Not only does mime enable the less vocal group members to be included in reminiscing, but it can also improve confidence in group situations and spark off memories in other learners.

Case study

Doris was a quiet member of a reminiscence group, who was excluded from a lot of discussions because of her hearing impairment. The reminiscence tutor found that one way to include her in sharing memories was to encourage her to demonstrate with mime such things as doing the washing. Doris's sometimes solemn expression would break into a big grin as she mimed these activities. She was also able to comprehend other group members better as they mimed their chosen activities.

Another way of using mime to share memories is to get people to act out doing the jobs they had when younger. This can be used as a game where people who don't know each other well guess what others did, or as a way of explaining what a particular job consisted of. Some learners feel uncertain when first faced with the prospect of miming in front of the group, but this is generally overcome by having a go. For mime to be used to best effect it is a good idea to stick to asking people to mime actions which they are very familiar with.

One group of physically and cognitively disabled learners made up and acted out stories using a selection of memorabilia chosen from a display. After experimenting with roles and storylines inspired by the memorabilia they scripted a short play with the tutor's assistance. The finished product provided the learners with a particularly strong boost to their confidence as they were able to see a tangible result from their efforts in making up and acting out the story over a number of weeks. In this particular case, items of memorabilia were used to teach characterisation, as each person was invited to choose items and build a character around them. The final storyline and theme of the play was based on learners' memories of the Second World War.

Workers at the Age Exchange Reminiscence Centre based in Blackheath in London have done a great deal of older people's theatre based on memories. One of these projects took place in Cromer on the Norfolk coast at a sheltered housing complex and day centre. Funding came mostly from the Department of Health, and the choice of venue was made after liaising with Adult Education. Benjamin Court was chosen as an ideal place to develop the project because the older people living there and attending the day centre, as well as the staff and volunteers, had already demonstrated their openness to new activities and ideas. This meant that Age Exchange could build on the activities already taking place. Two members of the Age Exchange team visited Benjamin Court on a fortnightly basis from January to April 2003, holding reminiscence groups and encouraging people to share their memories, later expressing them through art and drama. A stage backdrop full of visual representations of participants' memories was produced by the group. On the day of the performance, eleven people acted out their memories in front of an audience, whilst the backdrop expressed many more memories. Music and singing reflecting further memories were used throughout the performance. Around 50 older people were involved in the project.

Bernie Arigho of Age Exchange described confidence building as amongst the most significant benefits of using live theatre at Benjamin Court. The participants saw their memories being appreciated and valued as they brought enjoyment to others. Both the performance and the video made on the day meant that these memories could be shared with a much wider audience, thus enhancing the sense of their value. Bernie describes live theatre as having an immediacy providing a greater emotional impact than is possible when sharing memories in written form. Participants were given a lot of support throughout the project, and it was recognised that they were taking a risk by sharing their stories in a public way. However, this was 'healthy risk taking' because by exposing themselves publicly, participants were actually producing a profoundly moving performance which was greatly appreciated by others. This was a new way of working for Age Exchange, but it has proved to be a model of good practice which has been used again since. The older people also recognised the benefits saying that they would like more such activities.

Reminiscence and music

There has been an increasing amount of research over the past two decades into how music can improve learning. Webb and Webb (1990) list a number of beneficial effects of music on the mind and body:

- increases energy in the muscles and cells;
- influences the heartbeat;
- alters metabolism;
- reduces pain and stress;
- speeds healing and recovery in surgery patients;
- relieves fatigue;
- helps in the release and expression of emotions;
- stimulates creativity, sensitivity and thinking.

These effects are clearly beneficial when working with groups of older people who may suffer from high levels of fatigue and pain, and a slowed rate of metabolism. By using music in reminiscence sessions we can increase the levels of alertness, energy and concentration in our learners at the same time as stimulating their thoughts, creativity and memories. Music reduces stress (which inhibits concentration and learning) and aids relaxation (Jensen, 2000). There has been a variety of research into the kinds of music that enhance learning most, but in the context of reminiscence it is appropriate to use any music which the learners have indicated they enjoy. Until you get to know the learner group it is probably best to stay with the well-known favourites from the 1940s and 1950s, but learners in their 80s may have preferences ranging from Mozart to Madonna. As in everything else the key is to ask people what they like and not make assumptions based on stereotypes of older people.

Case study

Pat Sexton works with her husband Richard providing reminiscence social evenings based around music and dance. Together they sing and play the keyboard, reproducing music from the 1950s to the 1970s in which residents of sheltered housing schemes and residential homes are invited to join. The participation ranges from doing the 'Hand Jive' to getting up and dancing, with or without the assistance of care workers, as well as singing along to well known tunes. Some people stand at their walking frames and do the Twist, whilst others tap their feet to the music or clap in time. Pat has found that the music reaches parts of the brain that are untouched by the ordinary reminiscence groups she runs. She has seen people who hardly participate in discussions sing along for a whole evening. The benefits of these occasions include the mental and physical stimulation which motivates people to get involved and brings back memories of the fun they had dancing in the past. The more able groups make a complete social event of it by dressing up for the occasion, having their hair done and applying make-up. All these things help to restore and maintain skills they had in the past, and contribute to their enduring independence. Pat has found that music reaches everyone, even those with severe dementia, and that it makes people more willing to join in with reminiscing as they feel less threatened. The fact that she works in a team with her husband helps to create an atmosphere in which people interact with them and with each other, as they see the banter between Pat and Richard and respond with their own humour.

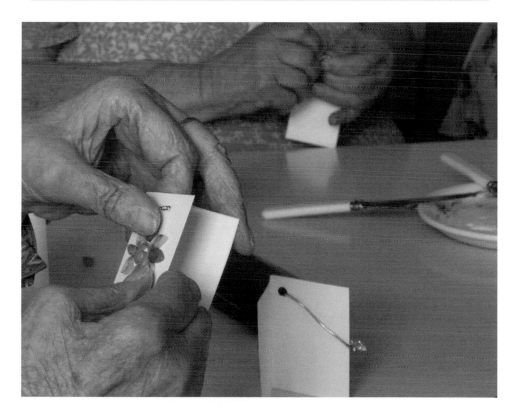

Case study

'Pabulum' is a charity based in Norwich which works with people with dementia. Since April 2002 they have been holding a monthly music group, known as Wroxy Music, in the village of Wroxham. This is attended by carers with their cared-for relative with dementia, and a number of volunteers. Pabulum has found that music is a useful communication tool, more readily accessible to people with dementia than ordinary reminiscence discussion groups. At Wroxy Music, participants play percussion instruments and sing, reaching the parts of the brain responsible for rhythm, which are less vulnerable to memory loss than those dealing with higher levels of cognition. Any signs of joining in through playing instruments or movement are encouraged by volunteers mirroring the action of group members, and participants who want to get up and dance are encouraged to do so. All these activities – singing, dancing, playing instruments, and interacting with others in a joint activity – reinforce social, cognitive and verbal skills.

Pabulum has also found that music is an effective means of enabling people to connect with their emotions and a powerful way of bringing about changes in mood, as well as relaxation. During the afternoons the group focuses on themes related to the time of year and seasonal celebrations, or a particular musical, such as South Pacific. Whatever the theme for the day, a craft activity is usually included, as well as part of the afternoon being given over to reminiscence with memorabilia on the chosen theme. The overall effect of a day spent at Wroxy Music is plenty of stimulation to mind and body, enhanced social interaction and a thoroughly enjoyable day out in which the person with dementia has been able to take part in activities alongside their carer, rather than always having things done for them. Of particular importance is that there is never any failure at Wroxy Music because activities are designed to be within the capabilities of all participants. This contributes to the feeling of well-being experienced by both carers and cared-for.

Reflection and application

1. Are there ways in which taking part in creative activities poses a particular challenge to you? If so, do you think the older people you work with would feel the same? How can you work together with others to overcome these challenges?
2. Do you have any creative skills which you could incorporate into reminiscence work? Are you aware of any such skills in older people you know, such as the ability to paint, write, act, sing or play a musical instrument?
3. Consider how creative activities could be used to enhance the expression of any minority groups you are familiar with. Are there people within your community who would benefit from opportunities to try out alternative means of expressing their cultural heritage?

Chapter 7

The role of Information and Communication Technologies

The role of Information and Communication Technologies

Computers, digital cameras, mini-disc recorders, along with other modern communication technologies, are increasingly used as part of recording and passing on memories in lifelong learning. Ten years ago there was a prevailing attitude of 'older people aren't interested in ICT' and comments such as 'I've got by all my life without it, I can continue to do so now' or 'I just can't understand computers; they frighten me; what happens if I press the wrong button?' were frequently heard from members of the older generations when offered the opportunity to learn about ICT. Much to the benefit of older people and those communicating and working with them, such attitudes are well on the way to being overcome. Older people living in 'Housing with Care' schemes in Norwich are enjoying using computers which have been made available for them to e-mail children and grandchildren who live some distance away, as well as making contact with old friends and long-forgotten relatives through 'friends-reunited' and 'genes-reunited' websites. These opportunities are repeatedly demonstrating the relevance of modern technologies to older generations, and many older people living in care have taken advantage of ICT training provided by adult education tutors and local charities.

Our main concern here is how ICT can be used to enhance the process of triggering and recording memories, not just for older generations but for people of any age, and how this in turn enriches learning experiences in and outside adult education groups. For many individuals, the Internet has become an invaluable resource in researching local and family history, providing information ranging from local myths and traditions, to photos of long-demolished landmarks and census information. Most regions of the country, if not the world, have websites detailing local history. In Norfolk there is a particularly useful website compiled by the Norfolk Library and Information Service which comprises photos from around Norfolk spanning several decades (see 'Picture Norfolk' via **www.norlink.norfolk.gov.uk**). Many reminiscence tutors have found such pictures invaluable as a source of triggers. After finding out where people originate from, or have lived and worked during their lives, pictures can be located on the Internet, and with permission, printed off and taken along to group sessions where they are used to trigger memories associated with these places. Where relevant photos do not exist on the Internet, and the locations are not too far away, tutors can also make good use of digital cameras in making visits and taking photos themselves. Home computers then grant instant access to large, clear photos of places as they are today, which can lead to fascinating group discussions on the changing use of buildings, fields, transport and waterways. Digital photography makes this possible at a price and speed which was not possible with conventional photography, as well as making it possible to produce A4-size photographs – more easily visible to those learners with visual impairments.

Many people have also found computers useful as a means of recording their own life history, which can then be passed on to children and grandchildren as a keepsake, complete with scanned photographs and explanations of their contents. This is all information which might otherwise have been lost, or difficult to record due to problems with writing by hand after the onset of conditions like arthritis and Parkinson's disease.

Community archiving using ICT

Throughout Norfolk, in market towns, villages and within special interest groups, groups of ordinary people have been getting together during the past six years to compile computer based archives of their local communities. Specially designed software exists to make this task easier, and within Norfolk, the principal one in use is COMMA (Community Multi-Media

Archiving). Norfolk Adult Education's 'Older People's Project' has led the way in introducing this software to groups wishing to create an archive which is accessible to all members of their communities. Support is also provided to these groups in the form of training in using the software and meetings where different groups can get together and discuss the progress they are making with their individual archives. There is great potential in this for learning from each other's mistakes and successes, as well as gaining encouragement from like-minded people. COMMA software is designed for use by people who are not computer literate, providing clear instructions at every stage of creating the archive, together with a straightforward method of presenting information on screen. Simple security measures exist so that the completed archive can be placed in a public place without unauthorised members of the public being able to add or erase entries. This has made it possible for COMMA Archives to be placed in local libraries in some instances.

The role that computer-based archiving has played in reviving local communities is explored in more detail in the next chapter. Here, we shall limit ourselves to a general overview of the value of using the COMMA software:

The value of COMMA

- All sorts of people can take part in creating a community archive using COMMA. You don't need to be confident with computers, or have any prior experience as the programme has been designed to be user-friendly.
- COMMA provides a way for groups of local people to work together. This includes intergenerational work as young people bring their familiarity with computers, whilst older

people bring their memories, photos and memorabilia. Older people's memories are valued and relationships built up between the generations.

- It is useful in widening participation amongst people who might not have seen either computers or local history as interesting. It brings history to life for younger people, and shows a relevant use for IT to older people.
- COMMA is accessible because it is easy to use and was designed for use by older people who may have no experience with computers. It therefore introduces people to ICT and helps them to develop their skills and confidence. These may then be transferred to other learning situations or everyday life.
- COMMA creates long-lasting images which anyone can access through libraries and museums. Archives can also be put on the Internet. There is no end to the archive as there is to a book, as it can be continually added to and reshaped with passing time. It is living history, giving an ongoing record of events in a community over decades or centuries.
- It attracts interest from a large number of people in the community as anyone can look at the history of places and people they know. This is likely to spark off other memories which can then be added, making the experience personal.
- Different aspects of local history can be linked together using 'Hotspots' and 'Storylines'. Hotspots can be used to show the history of different places (e.g. shops) or people. It is possible to follow whole families through several generations once the archive has been built up. COMMA archives can therefore be especially useful for family history research. The 'Hotspots' are also useful for remembering the names of people in old photos, which might otherwise be forgotten with passing time.
- Most people have photos relevant to the history of their community, but they are unlikely to want to give them away. With COMMA, photos can be copied and returned to their owners undamaged. This makes people more willing to take part. Once the photos are on the archive, reminiscences can be added to them, making them more widely available than when kept in a box at home. It removes the danger of archives being shut up in the attic where nobody can see them.

COMMA is a way of recording memories which has the potential for involving a wide cross-section of the community. The learning value exists not only for those involved in creating the archive, but also for anyone who views it. This has been made easier by the fact that it is possible to publish archives in the making on the Internet and in CD-ROM format, both of which offer further challenges to the archiving groups in terms of developing their ICT skills. For further information about COMMA software see **www.commanet.org**.

Exploring family history

There has been an explosion of interest in the United Kingdom over the past ten years in exploring family history. This has resulted in a vast range of websites which assist the process, together with the provision of adult education classes on how to research your family tree using the Internet. In some ways it could be said that this is a subject outside the remit of this book, as it is not strictly related to the memories of living people. However, not only is it clearly related to the subject of lifelong learning as families gather a growing body of knowledge about their descent, but many families have also found that the process of looking for ancestors has put them in touch with living relatives doing similar research – some of whom they did not know existed, and others with whom they had had no contact since childhood.

The case study of the research of retired couple, Richard and Jane, describes the process and some of the triumphs of exploring family history:

Case Study – Richard and Jane, exploring family history

'To us its about discovering who people were, where they lived, what they did and how the web of family relationships has led to us, here today, together with our children and grandchildren.

Our interest started when one of my sons began researching our family history. He came to see me to talk over what he had found, and I was fascinated to hear him talking of my grandparents, their parents and so on, going back several generations. Some of the things I already knew, and I was able to fill in a few details based on things I had experienced and stories I had heard as a child. My son later produced a CD of family photographs, going back to the beginning of the twentieth century, together with information about other ancestors going even further back.

It set me thinking about my own childhood and the people and events I could remember. I began to write down some of my memories and do some of my own researching. I learned about the availability of Civil Registration Records (the 'St Catherine's Index') and discovered that every city library has a copy of this on microfiche as well as the fact that I could research it on-line. You have to look through hundreds of pages sometimes before you find what you're looking for. I have found library staff very helpful in using the microfiche index. The 'St Catherine's Index' tells you when people were born, married and when they died. I have learned to link this with Census Records, which tell you what people did and where they lived. There has been a Census every ten years since 1841, apart from 1941, when the Second World War meant that there were too many displaced persons for the Census to be carried out. The information is interesting because you can picture whole households on a particular night, learning the occupation and age of each of them. I access the Census records either through local libraries or on-line, but have found that they are not always an entirely reliable source of information. The records show what the householder told the enumerator, who wrote down what they think they heard. This means that names can be misspelt, making them difficult to find when searching the Census Records. Also, not all enumerators were thorough in what they wrote, making estimates about ages and sometimes having handwriting which is a challenge to read. If the images have faded with time this adds to the difficulty of reading the records.

Other records of interest are apprenticeship records and parish registers, which are generally held in the archives of local authorities. We have also found old newspapers on microfilm useful for learning about the deaths and inquests of a few relatives who died in unusual ways. Even visiting cemeteries has provided us with new information on some of our ancestors, such as their occupation and the roles they played in their local communities.

We have found e-mail exceptionally useful in discussing our findings and our memories with relatives with whom we have re-established contact as a result of our research. Through longstanding exchanges of e-mails I have found that my own memories have been brought to life. For instance, I managed to find the e-mail address of one of my cousins who I had not seen for over fifty years. We have now exchanged several e-mails in which she has described coming to stay with my Grandmother as an evacuee during the war. I had completely forgotten this, but when she talked about it, it set off a whole train of memories about my Grandmother cooking stews in a cauldron over an open fire in the garden, and doing her washing in the same way (but using a different cauldron!). As a result of our exchanging reminiscences, my cousin has now started writing down her recollections of her wartime experiences.

We have gone on to meet some of the relatives we established contact with through the

Internet, and find that we have memories of mutual relatives in common with some of these people, even though we have never met them before. We have exchanged photos and used a scanner to copy these so that the original can be returned to its owner. We then pass these photos around our other relatives to ask whether they have any memories of the people or the occasion pictured. It has sometimes been fascinating to hear the range of different memories associated with the same photo. We have also become aware that memories of different people can sometimes conflict with each other. For instance there are a wide range of stories about how Jane's Great Grandfather died, with many older people within the family being absolutely certain that the story that they have heard is most certainly the correct one, with all the others being myths. Ultimately, inquest reports, found in the old newspapers on microfilm in libraries, can help to establish the truth, but it has been interesting to see how differently people remember the same thing. We have discovered what a subjective thing memory is.'

Reminiscence on the Internet

Coinciding with the 60th anniversary of the D-Day landings the BBC set up the 'People's War' website and invited people throughout the country to contribute their memories of the war. This could be done by the individuals themselves if they had access to the Internet, or through volunteers who were available throughout the country at such places as libraries, to record and input others' memories where necessary. Norfolk Adult Education's 'Older People's Project' saw this as a good opportunity to demonstrate to learners the value of sharing their memories on a wider scale and a team of reminiscence tutors visited older people in residential homes, their own homes and at special events in order to record their memories of the war. Over 100 memories have been recorded under Norfolk Adult Education's page on the People's War site. Some of the advantages of this approach to sharing memories have been found to be the special value it places on the memories, being associated with a BBC project and published in a format which can be accessed anywhere in the world by anyone with a computer. This has had a marked effect on the self-esteem of many older people who are encouraged by the fact that people still want to hear about their experiences. The older people themselves have stressed the importance of sharing their memories on this scale as part of generating understanding about what they lived through, and in the hope that it does not happen again. In the cases of some particularly frail people who have been able to share their memories in this way, the experience has had particular meaning and value for their families, who feel proud that their parents and grandparents are sharing their stories nationally. Stories which might always have had importance to individuals and their families are being given the value they deserve, by being seen as of interest to a much wider audience. In some cases, the Adult Education Service has been contacted by other organisations doing research into topics such as the British Red Cross or Japanese Prisoners of War, who have asked to do more detailed interviews with some of the contributors. At every stage of this process, older people are learning the value of their memories and the fact that they can be used to further the learning of others. To view the BBC People's War website go to **www.bbc.co.uk/ww2**.

Websites also exist locally where people can record their memories of Norfolk. One example is the site set up by Linda McAllister in 2003, originally as a way of publicising a genealogy search service. This has grown into a large and varied website with opportunities existing to reminisce about school days, wartime Norwich, working life and sport. There is a particularly extensive feature on the history of the Gorleston lifeboat, and platforms for discussion on working life at each of Norwich's main employers. The website provides a forum for Norwich people to share their memories of living and working in the city, whatever their age. (See **www.norfolkancestors.org** for further information on this site).

Conclusion

Throughout this chapter we have seen the many roles that ICT can play in enhancing the process of sharing and recording memories, and the way in which these processes have contributed to a growing awareness amongst older people that computers and other modern technologies are relevant to them. In the following chapter we shall look at how ICT has played a part, alongside other methods of sharing and recording memories, in reviving local communities.

Reflection and application

1. What are/were the significant industries in your local area? Do they have their own archives? What steps would need to be taken to begin sharing memories of the workforce with a larger audience? What would be the benefits to individuals and the community of beginning a computer based archive such as COMMA?
2. Carry out a search on the Internet to see what local websites exist which provide information about your area, its industries and history. Are there any significant gaps in the topics covered? If so, do you know anyone you could work with or encourage to fill that gap?
3. What services are available in your area to assist people who want to research local and family history? What might be the benefits to individuals and families of knowing more about their roots?

Chapter 8

The role of the past in reviving communities

The role of the past in reviving communities

This chapter uses the examples of two communities in Norfolk where reminiscence has played a part, alongside community archiving, in restoring a sense of community to a local area. In both cases, large numbers of people have become involved in the projects, either in a small way on a temporary basis or as a key member of the group over a longer period. The two community groups described are Ludham, a rural village in the east of Norfolk, and Sprowston, which, although retaining an identity as a separate community, has gradually become a suburb of the city of Norwich. In both cases, the local heritage and archiving groups have developed into wide ranging projects, which enable people with a variety of skills and interests to take part in recording local history and the memories of community members. The examples demonstrate the effectiveness of reminiscence and community archiving in getting a large section of local people involved in fulfilling a common purpose, and again emphasises the extraordinary resource represented by the memories of individuals and groups.

Ludham Archive Group

Ludham Archive group started off as a textile group, setting out to produce a map of the village to be displayed in the church. This has gradually expanded to involve a computer based archive, history talks and slide shows, as well as guided historical walks around the local area. The group holds suppers on a regular basis, where, as well as food being provided, slides are shown and an update given on the archive. Many more people come to these meetings than to the regular archiving meetings, as although they express an interest in the work being done they are not involved in it on an ongoing basis. About twenty people come to the regular planning, update and discussion meetings, while over forty people come to the slide shows and up to eighty to the suppers. The group has produced books, CD-ROMS, DVD's and postcards for sale. Two CD-ROMS showing material from the archive have been bought by many members of the community. This helps with financing the ongoing work, as well as spreading the word about the archive. The DVD, 'Village Chatter', contains audio-visual clips of local people reminiscing about village life over the years. This has proved to be very popular with current residents as well as those who have lived in Ludham in the past. Through appearing on 'Village Chatter' one lady described how she had re-established relationships with people she knew from her youth who had seen her piece and subsequently contacted her. Five booklets have been produced about local streets, the airfield and life in Ludham during the war with hundreds of copies of these books being sold. The archive group has also been involved in a local history weekend where they produced an impressive display in the church.

Funding has come from various sources over the years. North Norfolk District Council originally provided a grant to pay for a textile artist to provide advice and expertise in producing the village map. Further funding was obtained from 'Awards for All' to provide a computer, a scanner and a mini-disc recorder, as well as the printing of books. Later awards financed a projector so that slides could be shown from the computer archive at public meetings. Slide shows have included themes such as 'boats and boat-builders', 'farms', 'mills and millwrights' and 'aerial views of Ludham'. North Norfolk District Council awarded the group a competition prize, for involving so many local people in the project. They are gradually becoming self-sufficient through the production of CDs, DVDs and books.

Many members of the Ludham Archive group had had very little exposure to modern technology in the form of computers before becoming involved in the group. Once the need for training had been identified Norfolk Adult Education Service provided introductory courses in using computers in the church hall, which were attended by some group members.

The skills learned have been used by several members in typing up memories, and listing and indexing archive contents so that material can be found more easily. Some group members describe how they felt terrified of computers before joining the group and attending the adult education classes, but now have a great sense of achievement after learning to use software, gaining certificates and being able to get more involved in adding to and maintaining the archive. Group members with more experience with computers have provided support for the novices and helped them to grow in confidence about their abilities. One older gentleman, who made up his mind to have nothing to do with computers still uses ICT indirectly as the photos he has borrowed from village people have been scanned, enhanced and printed out, much to his delight. The computer novices in the group are now convinced of the effectiveness of ICT in providing the means of recording and preserving memories.

Members of the Ludham Archive Group describe having learnt a great deal about the village through the project. This has been a surprise to them, as in some cases they have lived there most of their lives, and thought they already knew everything there was to know! However, through talking to friends and neighbours about their memories they have found that there is always more to learn, and local people are more than willing to share their memories. One of the key things they have found is that it is important to record – either in writing or on audio equipment – the things that people tell them, as recording the exact words creates a much richer resource for others than can be held in their individual memories.

Ludham is a community partly divided by the fact that over half the villagers have come to live here in the past ten years. Taking part in the archive group has enabled longstanding members of the community to get to know these 'strangers', and many of the people actively involved in the project are newcomers. Those who are new to the village and part of the archive group have found that this is a very effective way of getting to know others, and becoming rapidly involved in village life. One lady described how, despite being a newcomer, she can walk through the village and speak to most people she sees, as a result of her involvement. The group feels that their work has been effective in bringing people together and they have discovered a network of blood and marriage relationships in the village which they were previously unaware of. As a result there is a growing sense of the Ludham community being more than a collection of individuals. For those who were more familiar with town life before coming to Ludham, learning about village life throughout the past century has been a revelation – largely because this rural location was slow to be reached by modern luxuries. The contents of the archive illustrate how much Ludham has changed over the past few decades, from a 'backwater with narrow roads' to a 'totally different, busy world' and this has been important in enabling newcomers to understand the history of Ludham and to feel part of the community. Group members describe it as a new thing for newcomers to become involved in village life, joining local clubs and wanting to learn about Ludham's history through the archive. There is also a feeling that the village as a whole has become more friendly through the involvement of these newcomers. The archive group's activities have helped to integrate the 'strangers' into the community even though they have no memories specific to Ludham life as they have been able to share their ICT skills with the group.

As well as getting to know village people, archiving has enabled participants to learn about the buildings in the village and the key members of the community in past times. This has contributed to a growing sense of togetherness, as newcomers do not change the village to suit their own needs, but become part of a continuous process of developing village life which is a story spanning centuries. Almost all the villagers approached for help with the archive have been willing to take part and have been interested in what is being done. Younger generations have shown a great deal of interest in what has been produced and are happy to contribute ideas, but tend to hold back from actually joining the archive group. Local schools have been involved through making parts of the community textile map. They also have their own mini-archive, contributed by the group, and this fits into National Curriculum studies which involve learning about the church, the village and wartime experiences. Interest has also been shown by people who have previously lived in the village and continue to identify themselves with Ludham.

Sprowston Heritage Group

Sprowston Heritage Group was started by a Community Education Officer working in partnership with the Adult Education Service, Youth and Community Service, and Sprowston High School. She recruited a small group of local men to set up a COMMA archive, using a computer borrowed from Adult Education's 'Older People's Project'. This small group of men grew, until the idea of having a wider heritage group blossomed by the year 2000.

The project has been funded by a Heritage Lottery Grant, and the current project co-ordinator has put into action the ideas of the heritage group including a tapestry showing the history of Sprowston, a community play and a 'reminiscence and research' group, in addition to the original COMMA Archive group.

The 'reminiscence and research' group publicises itself as an opportunity to find out about and talk about Sprowston in the past, and is attended by about 40 people on a regular basis. The group meets once a month and has close links with the COMMA Archive groups as opportunities are presented to record their memories and photos on the archive. The format in the past has been to have a speaker each month, but it has been found that this leaves lit-tle time for reminiscing. Group members have now expressed a desire to spend more time talking about their own memories. They also carry out their own research projects, visiting the Norfolk Records Office and writing booklets about what they discover.

Katy Carr, the current project co-ordinator described how the COMMA group consists mostly of men recording the history of brick yards, buildings, geographical structure and social history, while the women prefer to talk about pictures they took when younger which spark off their memories about families, friends and events. With this contrast in the aims and desires of the sexes the 'reminiscence and research' group provides a valuable alternative venue for the women to share their memories.

The archive group has gathered together over 1000 images which have been placed on computer. The main task now is to organise this material and find ways of using it effectively in demonstrations and talks. Work is beginning on an oral history project, and it is hoped that having recordings of local people reminiscing will enliven and diversify the use of archive material. The plan is for the oral history project to link directly to the COMMA archive, as well as being used to inform future community plays and making a record of the memories shared at the 'reminiscence and research' group.

Sprowston Heritage Group worked in partnership with a drama teacher at the Kett Sixth Form who was an experienced director in community work and made it part of the 'A' Level Curriculum for her students to join in with producing the community play. In September 2004, a group of adults who were largely new to the Heritage Group were recruited for the play. This included experienced amateur actors, as well as people who had no experience on the stage. In January 2005, a group of sixth-form students, with the help of members of the com-munity group, performed a play about life in Sprowston during the war which was written largely by the students, with community members playing minor roles. The next production was held in February in the local Lazar House, an appropriately historical setting. The wartime play was later expanded to be performed at Norwich Cathedral in July. This included many 'extras' in the form of students and the cathedral choir, singing wartime songs. There was a large cast and the performance was sold out, turning out to be a big success in terms of involving a large number of local people in a remarkable piece of moving historical drama.

The COMMA Archive was used to develop ideas and storylines for the play, and the drama teacher instilled the idea of Sprowston Heritage into her students as they wrote the script. The initial idea was taken from the 'Roll of Honour' of those from Sprowston who died in the war. Stories were written around their experiences and those of the women who were left behind.

The design of the Sprowston Heritage tapestry started in 2000 and was an ongoing project over six years. The tapestry consists of four panels covering the period from 1000 AD to the present. Trees at the side of the first panel diminish in subsequent panels to symbolise the fact that Sprowston has gradually changed from a wooded to a built-up area over the past millennium. The 'stitchers' gradually grew in confidence and worked busily until they finished the tapestry in the summer of 2006. Participation in this work has involved learning and developing a high level of needlework skills, and has included men as well as women.

There are 360 people on the project's database who have been involved in various aspects of the project through the past five years. A quarterly newsletter is produced providing news on each area of the project. On an ongoing basis there are eight people on the committee, about 20 involved in the tapestry, eight in the COMMA group and 20 in the play group. Members of Sprowston Heritage Group give talks to local school children and community groups, and the project has a high profile in the community through appearing at local fetes, adult education events and in the parish magazine on a regular basis. One of the big success-es of the project has been the way the members have worked in partnership with other groups, especially the High School. This is also seen as being important in securing the groups' future by providing continuity after funding for the co-ordinator's post ends.

The group has successfully provided the community of Sprowston with a voice within the Norwich area, and there has been a significant role for older citizens in this. Reminiscence has been a powerful tool in enabling people to feel connected to their community and their pasts. It has also broken down barriers between generations as older people have had opportuni-ties not only to talk to younger people but to work alongside them in producing the play. Individuals have benefited by growing in confidence, with one very timid man gaining enough confidence to perform on stage. It has established a social circle for many women who had not previously related to the existing community groups. They now enjoy being part of a group with a common purpose and feel that they can contribute something positive and use-ful through sharing their memories and taking part in the tapestry project. Those who are involved in the COMMA group have developed skills in ICT and have a growing interest in using the Internet and learning more about the potential of computers. The group has provided the structure and the social context in which this learning can take place. Talks have been given at venues as diverse as Gressenhall Museum and the University of East Anglia with group members becoming increasingly competent and confident in their delivery of presentations.

A key role for memories in reviving communities

These two case studies clearly indicate the significance and value of using the memories of local people in developing projects which draw communities together. In both cases, the projects started off as a small enterprise and have grown into something much bigger, involving hundreds of local people. Participation ranges from sharing and recording memories, to long-term commitment to needlework projects or creating computer archives. The learning which has taken place along the way includes growing confidence in skills involving using modern technology, public speaking and needlework, as well as working together in groups to turn the aspirations of the community members into reality. A willingness to work together is essential to the success of these projects, and results in people having a much stronger sense of purpose and belonging within the context of the local area. Working in co-operation with each other has itself involved the development of new social and group skills, and the benefits to both individuals and their communities are self-evident. The most significant thing about the success of these projects from the point of view of a reminiscence enthusiast is that they began with an interest in recording the past and are highly dependent on the memories of those who take part. Again, it is clear that memories play a key role in providing inspiration and motivation for learning, as well as being the richest resource available to those involved in the projects.

Reflection and application

1. Are there any groups living in your area that might benefit from having their own computer based Community Archive? This could be people from a cultural, religious or ethnic minority, or a particular village, town or area of a city.

2. Are there groups of people within your community who feel socially, economically or psychologically isolated from the majority of the population? How might working together to produce a Community Archive help to increase understanding and tolerance between diverse groups of people living in the same geographical area? How could you or others begin to work to bring this about?

3. In addition to the examples given in this chapter (e.g. needlework projects, videos, talks and drama), can you think of ways a community archiving project might expand to reach a wider range of people in your community?

Chapter 9

Reminisence with museums and libraries

Reminiscence with museums and libraries

As sources of information and knowledge, museums and libraries have always seen themselves as places of education. However, it has only been relatively recently that visitors have been seen as people who can add to the resources available, as well as draw on them. There are now many opportunities to share memories and experiences at museums and libraries, which are then added to databases available to the public or included in displays as oral or written reminiscences. Alongside this, museums and libraries are becoming more open to taking a facilitating role in the sharing of memories by developing a variety of reminiscence and archive projects. Some of those currently taking place in Norfolk are described in this chapter, which focuses on the 'Roots of Norfolk' museum at Gressenhall, the three social history museums in Norwich, and work being carried out at the museums and library in Great Yarmouth.

'Roots of Norfolk' at Gressenhall

Colly Mudie works for the Norfolk Museums and Archaeology Service as the Learning Manager at 'Roots of Norfolk' at Gressenhall. Her role is to provide and promote learning opportunities at the museum for everyone, from the cradle to the grave. The work being done with older people currently consists of a series of reminiscence days in May and September, developed in partnership with Norfolk Adult Education Service. This work was started about six years ago when an adult education tutor working with Colly recognised the potential of 'Roots' as a reminiscence venue. These days provide a special programme for older people, during which they look briefly at the museum and then join in with a reminiscence session where they talk about their own experiences using museum artefacts as a focus and trigger. The day finishes with a singalong session held in the chapel, which includes listening to and taking part in a number of old-time favourite songs facilitated by live entertainers. There have been up to 100 people a day coming to reminisce in this way. However, the museum staff and volunteers have found that a quality experience is more likely where the numbers are lower, with groups of about 50 seeming the most workable. The museum also offers individual reminiscence sessions for groups who request them.

'Roots' was started as a rural life museum and has substantial collections of agricultural implements which appeal to many older people. Norfolk has a long history as a centre of agriculture and memorabilia relating to farming can sometimes be a powerful trigger in stimulating memories. The museum is housed in an old workhouse building so there is a need for sensitivity in bringing older people into this environment as some have memories of times when it was actively used as a workhouse. Although the museum staff and volunteers have not been aware of this being a problem for visitors, the building does sometimes act as a trigger for recalling memories.

Reminiscence sessions are held in the kitchen of Cherry Tree Cottage, which is a 1940s agricultural labourer's cottage. There are many cooking implements within the room, and the range can be lit. Outside there is a cottage garden which provides further sensory stimulation. Within the workhouse building there is a 1950s lounge and kitchen area containing furniture and ephemera appropriate to the era. The site also has a working farm, and during reminiscence days a Suffolk Punch horse is brought up from the farm to the main museum courtyard. As a living object the horse triggers some profound memories, particularly in men who have been farm labourers, as they are able to touch and smell it, as well as feel its warmth and the magnificence of its sheer physical presence. Despite these environmental resources to aid reminiscence, the attraction of Roots and its effectiveness in promoting visitors' reminiscences is due as much to the relaxed atmosphere and the openness of staff, as to the collections themselves.

Volunteers, known as 'Mardlers' (from a Norfolk word meaning gossip) have been enthusiastic in developing the work with older people and have sought training in reminiscence to develop their skills. A consultation process is currently under way looking at the issues and agendas in working with older people, in order to develop a quality service for them in a learning environment. The value of reminiscence from the museum's point of view is that visitors are able to share their memories in a way which builds up the knowledge of staff and volunteers, adding to the museum's knowledge and resource base. The collection can thus be developed to reliably reflect the experience of older visitors at the same time as showing that those experiences and memories are valued. The reminiscence days provide an enjoyable, non-threatening experience for the older visitors, where physical as well as emotional and intellectual needs are acknowledged and met.

Carers are seen as an important part of the day as they can inform staff and volunteers about the interests of visitors and work in partnership with them. Colly also recognises the value of giving carers the opportunity to experience the cared-for visitors in a new way. They may learn more about their life histories as well as new ways of communicating with them through stimulating memories. For many carers it is a welcome break to be away from the environment of the care home, in a place where they too can share their memories, and perhaps find some previously unrecognised common ground with their clients.

Christine Walters, one of the Mardlers at Roots, sees the days as offering choices to the visitors which are often lacking in the lives of older people in care. There are opportunities for each individual to choose which spaces within the grounds to go into and whether to follow and share particular memory paths which are triggered in their minds. Such choices often become more and more restricted in later life, leading to passivity in many residents of care homes as they gradually cease expressing their own individuality. A reminiscence day at Gressenhall can have a powerful effect in bringing a greater level of autonomy into older people's lives as they are given opportunities to share a side of themselves which may be obscured by the daily routines within the care home.

Social history museums in Norwich

Hannah Maddox is the Curator of Community History at the three social history museums based in Norwich – Strangers' Hall, Bridewell Museum and the Carrow House Costume Collection. This is a post funded by 'Renaissance in the Regions' which is aimed at making collections and museums more accessible to a wider range of people. The social history museums are making significant steps towards broadening the accessibility of collections to older learners. This includes moving towards working in partnership with care homes and developing a reminiscence programme. Within this, there is a vision for doing more than just providing a service, by collecting memories and feeding them back into the museums' resources. There are plans for the longer term of engaging more with older male learners by gathering contributions from them for the working life collection through tailor-made sessions to access and record personal memories.

Hannah Maddox and other staff at the social history museums are keen to evaluate the learning that takes place, not just within the confines of the museums, but also beyond its walls. It is recognised that not all people learn through looking and reading and that the experience of holding and using memorabilia can lead to more consolidated learning as it brings home to people of all generations what it felt like to do particular jobs or live in certain environments. Plans for the future include introducing intergenerational discussions within the displays as well as outside the museums and developing a series of memory boxes which will be available for loan. Staff are currently looking at how these boxes can best deliver their full potential by considering suggestions that could be made to borrowers about how to use the collections.

At the Carrow House Costume Museum in Norwich a short series of reminiscence sessions has been held in order to gather memories from the public about the clothing they have worn throughout their lives. There are also plans for sessions in which memories will be shared about experiences of being taught sewing at school. The museum has been involved in active outreach to the general public during 'street sessions' when students working with the museum go out into the streets and photograph current fashions, at the same time as recording the public's thoughts and views on the clothes they wear today. This adds to the Costume Museum's collection of resources by adding a sense of how fashions are constantly changing, and highlights the fact that memories are not stuck in the past but are constantly evolving. The museum is essentially based in social history as the clothes people wear tell you a lot about that person – their socio-economic standing as well as their personality, and sometimes their occupation. The memories recorded make the whole costume collection more personal, intimate and relevant to visitors by providing information that ordinary people can relate to – both now and in the future. The skills necessary in this kind of work depend just as much on being able to draw people out and get them to talk about their own thoughts, opinions and memories, as on having detailed historical knowledge.

The ongoing and forthcoming work of the social history museums in Norwich is aimed at making museum collections more culturally and intellectually relevant to the public, by engaging their experience, memories and imagination in active learning. There are some tensions between this approach and the traditional way of doing things in museums, where visitors would look at and read about displays with little interaction or sensory stimulation other than visual.

Museums and libraries in Great Yarmouth

'Great Yarmouth Voices' is a COMMA-based oral history project which was started in 2003 and was linked to a Single Regeneration Budget funded outreach strategy at the time. It was also part of research undertaken for the 'Time and Tide' Museum in Great Yarmouth. The memories recorded on COMMA are themed around displays within the museum such as the fishing industry, the history of Great Yarmouth as a seaside resort, and wartime memories, as well as containing some general memories about life in Great Yarmouth. The collection of about 180 oral reminiscences was recorded and processed by a team of volunteers, and has been combined with visual images from the archive to create a comprehensive display which is used primarily on special event days. On these occasions, the COMMA archive is used not only as a trigger for reminiscing, but also as a way of encouraging Yarmouth people to come along and add their own memories to the archive. The project has become self-perpetuating, as each time it is used it triggers further memories in visitors to the museum, who then offer to add their own contributions. It is therefore an ongoing project which museum visitors and Great Yarmouth citizens can feel that they are a part of.

Staff at the museum have found that people enjoy telling their stories, recalling long-forgotten events triggered by the oral accounts and images stored on COMMA. It leads to much more interaction between visitors to the museum than traditional static displays, as well as more involvement with visitors for museum staff.

The Great Yarmouth museums are planning to take their use of COMMA and reminiscence to a further level by involving more groups and beginning to reach out to isolated older people living in the community. This is likely to involve working in partnership with the Adult Education Service and local libraries. There are also hopes of including younger generations in the project, by creating a record of life in Great Yarmouth today. One advantage of COMMA is that when it is stored on a laptop computer it can easily be taken out of the museum to interested people in the community, who might find the museum environment either physically or intellectually inaccessible.

Great Yarmouth Library Service obtained funding from the Single Regeneration Budget to create an archive of local residents' memories by interviewing people in residential homes for older people in the Great Yarmouth area. Pauline Mia worked on this project, visiting the residential homes and holding reminiscence groups on a regular basis over a fifteen month period. Pauline identified three groups of people who benefited from this work. Firstly, she felt that she herself benefited through carrying out work which was interesting and educational. She learnt new things about how various items of memorabilia had been used, gaining a glimpse through 'a window into the past'. As well as improving her interviewing skills and being able to draw people out more easily as time went on, she learned to use the technical equipment, such as a mini-disc recorder, digital camera and computer.

Secondly, Pauline saw benefits to the older people who took part in the groups. The quieter ones began to come out of themselves and grew in confidence as they found that their memories were valued by Pauline and the other group members. Self-esteem was raised and concentration spans grew, to the point where people with quite advanced dementia who rarely spoke would make short but meaningful contributions. Lastly, the homes themselves benefited, reporting that residents continued to interact at the enhanced level achieved within the groups long after Pauline left. Also, those residents who were more cognitively able would look forward to Pauline's visits and be in a better mood as the time of her visit approached.

Over 100 older people took part in reminiscence groups as part of this project with their memories being recorded onto mini-disc and then transcribed. The aim is to produce booklets of the memories for the residents of each care home as well as to create a database of memories using COMMA software, which will be available for use by schools and the public.

Again it is clear that as well as learning taking place within reminiscence groups, the memories shared can become a valuable resource which can be passed on to a wider group of people and used in a variety of ways. Not only can the knowledge be used to enhance the formal education of under-sixteen's within the National Curriculum, but by using computer databases of memories, information about everyday life in the twentieth century can be made available to the public through libraries and other community venues. One great asset of projects which draw on the memories of local people is that the memories have an enhanced relevance and immediacy. By reflecting on the experiences of real people, to whom these things really happened, history comes alive as an enjoyable and engaging subject.

Summary

Each of these case studies highlights some essential points about the use of reminiscence in museums and libraries:

- It is now being recognised by an ever-widening group of people that older people's memories represent a tremendous resource in themselves;
- While visitors to museums and libraries can benefit from the information stored there, there is now a much greater awareness and willingness amongst cultural services to see visitors as a resource who can contribute their memories to the museum or library's store of knowledge;
- People of all generations who visit museums and libraries are no longer just passive recipients of a 'service', but are becoming actively involved in displays and sources of information;
- Through the use of reminiscence the communication barriers between cultural services' staff and the public are being broken down so that as visitors' reflections and contributions to collections are valued, staff are seeking and finding ways of speaking their language. This is opening up museums and libraries to a wider range of people as collections become something they can relate to and which therefore seem relevant to their lives.

Reflection and application

1. What are the advantages to museums and libraries of seeing visitors as a source of information and knowledge? What are the benefits to the visitors of these establishments taking this approach?
2. What potential is there for museums, libraries, Social Services and adult education services in your area working together in partnership to achieve greater fulfilment and satisfaction for their clients, learners and visitors?
3. How far have your local museums and libraries moved towards valuing the memories of their visitors? How could greater accessibility and involvement of the public in these facilities be encouraged?

Chapter 10

Good practice in working with memories

Good practice in working with memories

Throughout this book we have looked at a variety of ways in which learners' memories can be used to enhance teaching and learning throughout the lifespan. Numerous examples have been given which illustrate the rich resource represented by these memories, and the value of drawing on the experience and knowledge of older learners. In this final chapter, a number of suggestions are made regarding the practicalities of organising and running reminiscence activities. We also present a ten-point guide to good practice that should inform all our interactions with learners in this kind of work. Many of these points are common to good practice in all adult education work, but they are repeated here because their importance in maintaining personhood and respect in our relationships with learners cannot be emphasised enough.

Putting it into practice – reminiscence groups for older people

Advance planning and preparation is essential to success in reminiscence work. It is therefore important to develop guidelines on issues relating to the size of the group, number and length of proposed sessions, and selection criteria for participants, well before the first meeting. While an ongoing group is more likely to provide lasting benefits for participants, there may be financial constraints which determine how long input can be maintained with the same group of learners at the same venue. For instance, funding may be based on the number of learners participating at some point during an academic year, rather than on the length of the course or number of hour's duration. Service providers need to be clear from the start as to how many sessions they can provide for each group of learners, and how large a group needs to be, in order to meet funding criteria. The aims of individual groups will be determined by the proposed length of courses and the size of the group. For instance, a small group meeting for an entire academic year may plan and execute a project based around recording their memories and developing art, craft, ICT and literacy skills, whereas a large six week group may be limited to enhancing speaking and listening skills.

The ideal group size depends largely on what the purpose of the group is and the extent and nature of learners' disabilities. Where extensive one-to-one input is required from the tutor, groups will need to be limited to six to eight participants, and even with a group this small it may be necessary to employ a learning support assistant to work with learners with more profound disabilities. Where a group consists largely of people who are able to respond and participate without individual assistance, the maximum group size is likely to be twelve to fifteen learners. However, the author has worked with groups of up to twenty-five learners where there have been at least three volunteers to assist. In residential and day care settings, care assistants and activity organisers are often willing to take part. This should be encouraged where possible as it means that the benefits gained in the group can more easily be used to inform daily activities and individual care planning. Where this is not possible, or to enhance community involvement, volunteers might be recruited. The use of volunteers in learning activities is explored by Janet Swinney (2005) in Volunteers and Volunteering (see references). To summarise, group size will be determined by factors such as:

- funding criteria;
- the proposed purpose of the group;
- the abilities of group members.

In reality, it is not always possible to achieve the ideal group size, but consideration should be given to the ethics of running a group where participants may not benefit sufficiently to

justify the effort they put into attending and taking part. Although funding criteria may tempt service providers to recruit as many learners as possible, it is unethical to run groups where the organisation makes a profit but benefits to learners are minimal.

Selecting participants

Key factors determining who participates in reminiscence groups in residential, nursing and day care settings include the following:

- *The tutor's knowledge, experience and skills in reminiscence:* Before embarking on running a reminiscence group it is essential that tutors acquire some training in reminiscence. Norfolk Adult Education's 'Older People's Project' delivers a Level 3 OCN qualification for people working or wishing to work in this area. This course provides the knowledge, skills and experience necessary for engaging in regular structured reminiscence work with older people. There are also numerous providers of introductory courses throughout the UK, through which carers can gain information and knowledge on the basic skills required to begin reminiscence work. Age Exchange (see Resources) has a regular programme of inspiring training as well as publishing a number of useful books on the subject.

- *Knowledge, skills and experience of the tutor in working with older people:* Communicating with older people with disabilities such as dementia and dysphasia requires skills which can best be gained through practical experience. Dementia awareness courses are generally available throughout the UK, often provided by local branches of Age Concern or the Alzheimer's Society. The 'Approaches to Reminiscence' course provided by Norfolk Adult Education Service includes training on dementia and other disabilities frequently occurring in later life (such as visual and hearing impairments). It is also useful to have an understanding of twentieth-century social history, and how British culture and society have developed over the past hundred years. This avoids offence being caused through modes of dress and attitudes from tutors which may shock people whose social values were laid down before the sexual revolution of the 1960s. Ideally, however, the tutor would not express her own attitudes and values at all, as the focus of reminiscence is on the experiences and life stories of the group members.

- *Purpose and size of the group:* Individual factors such as personality, confidence and communication skills, will determine whether learners function best in small or large groups. Likewise, individual interests and preferences may influence whether potential participants wish to join groups focusing on different reminiscence activities. Some people may wish to limit their participation to talking and listening, while others are keen to try out creative activities or ICT. To some extent participants may therefore be self-selecting, although it is always good to encourage potential learners to expand the boundaries of their interests, skills and experience.

- *Reasons for excluding potential learners from reminiscence group work:* There are some circumstances when even if a person wishes to join a reminiscence group it is not necessarily advisable for them to do so. This may include people who are unable to respond sensitively to the needs of others, for example, a minority of people who regularly voice their negative opinions and may therefore inhibit the participation of other group members. Whether to include people who, because of agitation or dementia, are unable to sit still or stay in the room for the length of the group, may depend on the level of experience and confidence of the tutor. Exclusion and inclusion criteria will generally be developed with experience of what it is possible to achieve with groups of different sizes and participants of different abilities. To some extent it is a matter of what the tutor feels comfortable with and the degree of expertise of any assistants. The author frequently involves people described as 'wanderers' in reminiscence activities, who subsequently benefit from inclusion, sometimes to the surprise of other group members and care staff. It could be argued that far from being disruptive, such participants enhance the experience and achievements of a group through enabling members to work alongside others to whom they had previously ascribed little value. However, there are occasions when including agitated people in groups can prove disruptive, as does working with those who dominate discussions despite being asked to give others a chance to speak. It is advisable to work in smaller groups (two to four people), or on a one-to-one basis, with those who do not function well in a larger group. This may be the limit of what they can achieve, or it may in time lead to them participating more effectively in a larger group.

Length of sessions

When deciding how long a reminiscence session will last, it is always best to work on the principle of leaving learners wanting to come back for more, rather than exhausting them by taking them to the limits of their concentration and energy reserves, which may deter them from attending again. For this reason it is advisable to limit the duration of sessions to one hour for the more able learners, or as little as half an hour for those with difficulty concentrating on activities and discussions or staying in the room. In order to overcome the impracticalities of a tutor attending a venue to deliver such a short session, two or three small groups might be held at the same venue on one afternoon, with different people participating in each group.

Working with people with dementia

Modification of working practice, pace of sessions and learning activities will usually be necessary when working with groups comprised mostly of people with dementia. Effective communication is paramount, together with a willingness to value participation at any level. The following principles are useful in considering how to facilitate such a group:

- Make sure the environment is conducive to communication and that there is no other activity in the room. Avoid rooms where people are coming in and out. This may be difficult to organise in some residential or day care settings where the only room available for groups is the main lounge. It is therefore important to make staff aware of the need to avoid distractions for the duration of the session. It may seem an obvious point, but it can be helpful to ask staff to refrain from bringing the tea trolley round in the middle of the group! Make arrangements for refreshments to be available either at the beginning or end of the session. Similarly, care staff might be asked to provide group members with assistance in using the toilet before you arrive in order to avoid delays at the start of the session or interruptions during it.

- Make sure that you are calm and not under time pressure. Give group members your full attention – communicating with people with dementia can take a lot of effort and be tiring.

- Ensure your facial expression and body posture are reassuring and relaxed. People with receptive aphasia may pay particular attention to non-verbal communication.

- Identify yourself by name, and use group members' names when addressing them. Some people with dementia will recognise you enough to know that they have seen you somewhere before, but may not remember exactly who you are, what your role is or in what context they have met you. With more advanced memory difficulties they may deny ever having met you or having previously taken part in a reminiscence group. It is important not to argue the point as this will set up a situation of confrontation with the person. The best approach is to focus on the present and ask whether they would like to take part in the group on this occasion.

- Speak in a straightforward manner but avoid being patronising. Always endeavour to maintain the dignity of your group members.

- Allow time for individuals to understand what you are saying. Even with moderate dementia it can take a significant length of time to process information. Make sure they understand before you move the discussion on.

- Communication is a two-way process, and you need to be alert to pick up clues and prompts. Do not be afraid of long pauses and do not jump in and complete sentences for people while they are still in the process of formulating them. Listen for what is being said 'behind the words'. People with dementia may sometimes speak metaphorically.

- Do not assume that a person does not understand just because they do not respond immediately. It might be that they have not understood, or alternatively they may not want or be able to respond.

- Use short sentences and do not carry double messages in them. 'Would you like to hold these butter pats and show me how they were used?' should be divided up into two distinct sentences and the first one dealt with before the second is introduced.

- If possible, illustrate what you are saying. Use your hands and body language to support your words and meaning. Make sure your illustrations match your words – don't show a photo of A whilst talking about B.

- Even if their thought processes or use of words are mixed up, you may still be able to follow what a person is saying. Don't feel that you have to correct mistakes even when they have totally misunderstood you or responded inappropriately. It can undermine a person's confidence to constantly be corrected.
- Adopt a kind of 'poetic awareness'. If you don't understand what a person has said to you, mentally add 'like this in some way' to what has been said. Don't get hung up on the literal meaning of words!
- People with dementia sometimes have difficulty finding specific words which can be frustrating for both them and the listener. It might be helpful to encourage them to describe what sort of thing they are talking about, or what it looks like or is used for, in order for them to communicate their meaning more easily.
- Adopt the individual's frame of reference rather than working from your own. They may be operating mentally in a different time zone in which what they are saying would make sense. Try to see things from their point of view.
- Slow down and go at their pace. Don't expect them to adapt to your usual speed of operating.
- Acknowledge the obstacles to communication and seek to find a way through them. The person you are working with may have spent months or years being ignored or misunderstood and it can take time for them to tune in to using their communication skills again.
- Treat everything as an attempt to tell you something.
- Accept the person as they are.
  (Adapted from Goldsmith, 1996: 58–9)

The reflective practitioner

As in all group leadership and adult education teaching it is essential, if the skills of tutors are to develop, to evaluate each reminiscence session and reflect on the progress both they and their learners are making. This should be done soon after the session in a written format, covering the points suggested in the yellow panel.

What is evaluation?

The process of evaluating a reminiscence session involves asking yourself and your co-workers questions about how the session went and how it could be improved. It also involves acknowledging good practice and thinking about how you could build on this in future sessions. If things went wrong, this is your opportunity to think about why they went wrong and consider what you would do differently next time.

Why evaluate?
- In order to recognise and record the value of the work you are doing.
- To measure the quality of participation and the effect this has on everyday well-being.
- As part of considering how to improve future sessions.
- It involves the learners in giving feedback and expressing their opinions.

What should be evaluated?
- The amount of participation by every individual in the group – how could you make your reminiscence activities of wider appeal?
- Type of participation by each person – was their participation typical of them? How could you get them to take part more actively?
- The benefits of participation to individuals.

In addition to this evaluation process it is useful to spend time with other reminiscence workers or a supervisor, reflecting on the benefits and barriers to your work, and discussing ways of advancing your skills as well as those of your learners. Discussion with interested colleagues is useful not only for increasing your understanding of reminiscence work, but also for gaining encouragement and support in carrying out what can at times be quite demanding work. Norfolk Adult Education's 'Older People's Project' holds regular tutor development days at which ideas and successes are shared and difficulties in the work discussed. Most tutors find this a highly valuable process in expanding the range of activities and techniques they use in their work. It is also a way of recognising and encouraging good practice. In addition, reading around the subject is a useful activity in encouraging the growth of knowledge, skills and ideas. A number of books are recommended at the end of this text which can be read individually and/or discussed with interested colleagues.

Guide to good practice
Good practice is essential in working with learners' memories, firstly because they are so closely related to people's sense of well-being and identity, and secondly because the work will be more effective where learners feel that they and their contributions are valued by the tutor and other learners.

Ten-point guide to good practice in memory work

1) Give learners your full attention when they are speaking, indicating through verbal and non-verbal signals that you are listening to what they are saying. Ask open quetions to lead them into a greater level of description of the events and feelings that they remember.

2) Be willing to be challenged in your existing beliefs about the past, by remembering that all memories are subjective. The learner has knowledge of how they perceived and experienced events, and this may differ from commonly accepted perceptions of history. The tutor is not in a position to say that a learner did not experience something which they said they did.

3) Sharing of memories will be done at a deeper level if the tutor and other learners maintain a non-judgemental stance. Agreeing ground rules at the start of a session will help to foster an atmosphere of acceptance.

4) Except where permission is given to share memories more widely, confidentiality should be maintained within the group. Learners, as well as the tutor need to know this if open communication is to take place.

5) Create a comfortable learning environment, establishing rapport with the learners from an early stage and showing that as a group facilitator you can be trusted to value and respect people's memories. Learners will not move on to higher levels of participation and self-expression unless they feel safe within the group.

6) Learners should never be manipulated or coerced into talking about their memories. Choice must be maintained and respected, as part of empowering them and enhancing their autonomy. This is of particular importance when working with learners living in residential homes, where opportunities to make individual choices may have been reduced. Some participants may choose to listen rather than to talk. This is still participation and their choice should be respected. In many cases, learners who have been allowed to sit and listen for the first session will participate more actively once they feel comfortable in the group.

7) Tutors and facilitators need to be sensitive to learners' moods and other things which may be going on in their lives which will affect their ability to participate and concentrate. Memories will be affected by current mood, and if an individual is feeling unhappy it might be that all they can remember from the past is similar unhappy events. Be careful not to label people on the basis of how they appear, behave and share on particular occasions. There may be reasons for their attitudes which you know nothing about.

8) Older learners should be seen as individuals, with each individual having distinctive needs, likes and dislikes. It is a fallacy that 'the elderly' are a homogenous group who all have similar needs and behaviours. It is especially important to bear this in mind when working with people with dementia, who suffer more than most from being seen as similar to one another. This is partly because it can be more difficult for them to express their individuality once cognitive impairment leads to difficulty in verbal communication.

Linked to this is the fact that every individual has a preferred learning style and will respond better to different approaches to teaching and learning. For this reason it is essential to use a variety of teaching styles and methods, and to note the effectiveness of each with individuals.

9) When beginning a memory-based project with a group of learners, tutors and facilitators should resist the temptation to have a fixed idea of what will be achieved by the end. Until you get to know the group members, it will be impossible to predict the style or content of learning. It is also important to consider the process of taking part in a project as equally, if not more important than any final product. For some people, simply participating in an activity is a major achievement and putting pressure on them to create a specific product may be inappropriate. Be open to where the learners lead, playing a role in applying a general structure to sessions without specifying the content. Until you know what learners have experienced, and what memories they want to express and record, you cannot determine the direction of the work. Again, it is a matter of giving learners choice.

10) Tutors and facilitators working with older learners and with people's memories in general, need to develop qualities in their approach to teaching such as openness to others, creating a non-threatening environment and being able to go at an appropriate pace for learners. Memory work is by nature learner-centred and learner-directed, and when undertaken with skill and sensitivity can lead to impressive projects and achievements, as demonstrated throughout this book.

It only remains to say: enjoy your work, and keep listening to your learners. They have a lot to offer!

Reflection and application

1) Outline your existing knowledge, skills and experience in carrying out reminiscence work or working with groups of older people. How might you develop your abilities in these areas? Do opportunities exist locally for you to receive training, or will you need to look further afield?

2) Do you know anyone else interested in, or working in this area? Arrange a meeting with interested colleagues to discuss your ideas for beginning or developing reminiscence work.

3) Consider ways in which you will ensure adequate supervision, support and opportunities to develop your skills and knowledge once you are engaged in reminiscence work.

4) How might you extend your experience and skills in working with people with dementia? Do you feel confident about working with people with this variable and complex condition? If not, how might you gain the confidence you need?

References

Alzheimer's Society (2003), Information Sheet 401: 'What is Alzheimer's Disease?

Argyle, M. (1983) *The Psychology of Interpersonal Behaviour,* Penguin.

Bender, M., Bauckham, P and Norris, A. (1999), *The Therapeutic Purposes of Reminiscence,* SAGE Publications

Best, S., Griffiths, J. & Hope, T. (2000) *Active Sociology,* Pearson Education Limited

Bond, J., Coleman, P. & Peace, S. (eds) (1993), *Ageing in Society,* Sage Publications

Bornat, J. (2002a) 'Reminiscence and Oral History: Comparisons Across Parallel Universes' in Webster J.D. and Haight, B.K. (2002) (eds) *Critical Advances in Reminiscence Work,* New York, Springer Publishing Company

Bornat, J. (ed) (2002b) *Reminiscence Reviewed: perspectives, evaluations, achievements,* Open University Press

Butler, R. (1963) 'The life review: an interpretation of reminiscence in the aged' in *Psychiatry: Journal for the Study of Interpersonal Processes* 26;1: pp 65-76

Buzan, T. (2001) *The Power of Creative Intelligence,* Thorsons

Carlton, S. and Soulsby, J. (1999) *Learning to Grow Older and Bolder,* NIACE

Coleman, P. (1993), 'Adjustment in Later Life, in Bond, J., Coleman, P. and Peace, S. (eds) (1999) *Ageing in Society: An introduction to Social Gerontology* (2nd Edition), SAGE publications in association with The British Society of Gerontology and the Open University.

Dench, S. and Regan, J. (2000) *Learning in Later Life: Motivation and Impact,* Department for Education and Employment, Institute of Employment Studies. (Research Report RR183)

Erikson, E. (1980) *Identity and the Life Cycle,* Norton

Gibson, F. (1998) *Reminiscence and Recall: A guide to good practice* (2nd Edition), Age Concern England

Gibson, F. (2004) *The Past in the Present: Using Reminiscence in Health and Social Care,* Baltimore, Health Professions Press

Goldsmith, M. (1996) *Hearing the Voice of People with Dementia: Opportunities and Obstacles,* Jessica Kingsley Publishers

James, K. (2001) *Prescribing Learning,* NIACE

Jensen, E. (2000) *Brain-Based Learning,* The Brain Store

Kitwood, T. (1997) *Dementia Reconsidered – the person comes first,* Open University Press

Levinson, D.J. (1978) *The Seasons of a Man's Life,* Ballantine Books

Lindeman, 1926, *The Meaning of Adult Education;* cited in Smith, M.K. (1996, 2001) 'Lifelong Learning', *the encyclopaedia of informal education,* www.infed.org.lifelonglearning/-life.htm , accessed February 28, 2005)

Longworth, N. and Davies, W.K. (1996) *Lifelong Learning,* Kogan Page Ltd

Minton, D. (1997) *Teaching Skills in Further and Adult Education,* City & Guilds / Thorsons

Ratey, J. (2001) *A User's Guide to the Brain,* Abacus

Rogers, C. (1967) 'The Interpersonal Relationship in the Facilitation of Learning' in Kirschenbaum, H. and Henderson, V.L. (1989) *The Carl Rogers Reader,* Constable.

Rogers, C. (1977) 'The Politics of Education' in Kirschenbaum, H. and Henderson, V.L. (1989) *The Carl Rogers Reader,* Constable

Sargant et al (1997) *The Learning Divide: A Study of Participation in Adult Learning in the United Kingdom.* NIACE

Sperry, R. (1968) 'Hemisphere disconnection and unity in conscious awareness', *American Psychologist* 23, 723-33

Swinney, J. (2005) *Volunteers and Volunteering,* NIACE

Thompson, P. (2000) *The Voice of the Past* (3rd Edition), Oxford University Press

Webb, D. and Webb, T. (1990) *Accelerated Learning with Music,* Accelerated Learning Systems

Further resources

Books

Bruce, E., Hodgson, S. and Schweitzer, P. (1999) *Reminiscing with People with Dementia: A Handbook for Carers*, published by Age Exchange for the European Reminiscence Network

Coppock, L. (1995) *Material Pleasures: Creative ways of using fabric*, Belair Publications Ltd

Hubalek, S.K. (1997) *I can't draw a straight line: bringing art into the lives of older adults*, Health Professions Press, USA.

Melville, S. (1997) *Crafts for All Abilities: Simple projects for a wide range of skills and ages*, Search Press Ltd.

Osborn, C. (1993) *The Reminiscence Handbook: ideas for creative activities with older people*, Age Exchange – this is an irreplaceable guide to running reminiscence groups, providing a wealth of ideas for activities.

Parsons, V. and Parsons, G.M. (1998) *Simple Expressions: Creative and Therapeutic Arts for Older People in Long Term Care*. Venture Publishing.

Schweitzer, P. (1993) *Age Exchanges: Reminiscence projects for children and older people*, Age Exchange – a useful guide to intergenerational reminiscence work.

Schweitzer, P. (Ed.) (1995) *Making memories matter: Reminiscence and inter-generational activities*. London: Age Exchange.

Schweitzer, P. (Ed.) (1998) *Reminiscence in dementia care*. London: Age Exchange for European Reminiscence Network.

Schweitzer, P. (Ed.) (2004) *Mapping memories: Reminiscence with ethnic minority elders*. London: Age Exchange.

Schweitzer, P. (2006). *Reminiscence theatre: Making theatre from memories*. London: Jessica Kingsley.

Sim, R. (1997) *Reminiscence: Social and Creative Activities with Older People in Care*, Winslow Press

Internet resources

www.24hourmuseum.org.uk – useful reminiscence resource

www.active4life.me.uk – author's website

www.alzheimers.org.uk – Alzheimer's Society

www.bbc.co.uk/ww2 – BBC People's War website

www.classic-british-cars.com – useful reminiscence resource

www.commanet.org – information on COMMA software

www.costumegallery.com – useful reminiscence resource

www.fiftiesweb.com – useful reminiscence resource

www.historic-uk.com – useful reminiscence resource

www.homesweethomefront.co.uk – useful reminiscence resource

www.norfolkancestors.org – Norfolk based reminiscences

www.norlink.norfolk.gov.uk – route to 'Picture Norfolk'

www.reelclassics.com – useful reminiscence resource

www.seniorsnetwork.co.uk – useful reminiscence resource

www.vintagebroadcasting.org.uk – useful reminiscence resource

All websites accessed 14 March 2007.

Useful addresses

Norfolk Adult Education Service – Older People's Project
Wensum Lodge
169 King Street
Norwich
NR1 1QW
Tel: Margaret Plummer 01603 306579 or Jenny Zmroczek 01603 306584

The Older People's Project provides reminiscence and other activities for older learners, as well as training for care staff and others interested in developing their skills in working with older people. In addition, Jenny Zmroczek is the project co-ordinator of the ARCH Project, facilitating community archiving in Norfolk market towns.

Age Exchange:
The Reminiscence Centre
11 Blackheath Village
London
SE3 9LA
Tel: 0208 3189105

Age Exchange provides a good quality service of speakers, course leaders, books and materials designed to support and encourage reminiscence work.

Help the Aged
207-221 Pentonville Road
London
N1 9UZ
Tel: 0207 2781114
(Publishers of 'Recall')

Winslow Press
Goytside Road
Chesterfield
S40 2PH
Tel: 0845921 1777

Winslow Press is a publisher of a variety of materials and books which may be useful in reminiscence.

East Anglian Film Archive
The Archive Centre
Martineau Lane
Norwich
NR1 2DQ
Tel: 01603 592664

The East Anglian Film Archive has produced a number of videos on life in the region which are available to buy. These can be a great stimulus for reminiscence. Please contact them for a list of videos for purchase.

Past Perfect
Lower Farm Barns
Bainton Road
Becknell
Oxon
OX6 9LT
Tel: 01869 325052

Past Perfect produces and sells tapes and CD's of digitally re-mastered music from the past. They can provide you with a catalogue